/ 50

Recipes
from an
American
Herb
Garden

Text and Photographs by

MAGGIE
OSTER

MACMILLAN PUBLISHING COMPANY
NEW YORK

MAXWELL MACMILLAN CANADA
TORONTO

MAXWELL MACMILLAN INTERNATIONAL
NEW YORK   OXFORD   SINGAPORE   SYDNEY

For my mother, Lucille Houpt Oster,
gracious, gifted, and giving and still my favorite cook

My thanks to the many people who have generously shared their kitchens, gardens, and ideas, especially my parents, George and Lucille Oster; the members of the Kentuckiana Unit of The Herb Society of America; Betty Manning, Stream Cliff Herb Farm, Commiskey, Indiana; Ellen Grinsfelder, The Inn at Cedar Falls, Logan, Ohio; Richard Hodges; Bloomington, Indiana, Farmers Market; Conner Prairie, Noblesville, Indiana; Locust Grove, Louisville, Kentucky; Huntington Botanical Gardens, San Marino, California; Filoli, Woodside, California; and Calloway Gardens, Pine Mountain, Georgia.
For their significant roles in this book, my gratitude to Pam Hoenig, Jan Melchior, Tom Fiffer, Marta Hallett, Linda Winters, Josey Ballenger, and everyone else at Running Heads. Each in his or her own way has given much to conveying my sense of joy in herbs, food, and the American countryside.

A Running Heads Book

Copyright © 1993 by Quarto Inc.

Macmillan Publishing Company
866 Third Avenue
New York, NY 10022

Maxwell Macmillan Canada, Inc.
1200 Eglinton Avenue East, Suite 200
Don Mills, Ontario M3C 3N1

Typesetting: Cast of Characters / Color Separations: Fine Arts Repro
Printed and bound in Hong Kong by Leefung–Asco Printers Limited

Macmillan Publishing Company is part of the Maxwell Communication Group of Companies.

Library of Congress Cataloging-in-Publication Data

Oster, Maggie.
Recipes from an American herb garden / Maggie Oster.
p. cm.
Includes index.
ISBN 0-02-594025-2
1. Cookery (Herbs)   2. Cookery, American.   3. Herb gardening.
I. Title.
TX819.H4088   1993   92-31370
641.6'57--dc20   CIP

Macmillan books are available at special discounts for bulk purchases for sales promotions, premiums, fund-raising, or educational use. For details, contact:

Special Sales Director
Macmillan Publishing Company
866 Third Avenue
New York, NY 10022

10 9 8 7 6 5 4 3 2 1

Recipes from an American Herb Garden
A Running Heads Book, Quarto Inc., The Old Brewery, 6 Blundell Street, London N7 9BH

Creative Director: Linda Winters / Designer: Jan Melchior / Senior Editor: Thomas G. Fiffer
Managing Editor: Jill Hamilton / Production Associate: Belinda Hellinger

CONTENTS

I grew up on a family farm where meals were always a celebration, with the food prepared, eaten, and praised with pleasure. Almost all of it was homegrown and fresh from the garden or from reserves stashed in canning jars and the freezer. Family vacations driving around the country to historic sites and gardens provided a joyful opportunity to sample indigenous foods. As an adult my wanderlust has taken me to all fifty states. On these sojourns I constantly explore groceries, produce stands, farmer's markets, garden centers, restaurants, public and private gardens, and home kitchens.

What I've seen happen in the last twenty years is a great increase in the availability of herbs for growing in the garden and of common herbs offered fresh year-round in groceries. Simultaneously, Americans have become sophisticated eaters, enjoying a diversity of readily obtainable foods. Ethnic cooking and ingredients are now widely familiar and have taken on an American character. Added to this are a heightened awareness of and concern for healthful food.

Most of our herbs have a long heritage in both America and other parts of the world. They are at once of ancient civilizations and the most innovative of twentieth-century cuisine. Herb gardens consistently offer timeless, tranquil, unaffected beauty, connecting us to our past with their redolent scents and flavors. Because of my own heritage I have a strong sense of place, of the old ways, of food personally nurtured and lovingly prepared and eaten. What herb gardens and cooking with herbs give each of us is a link with that sense, even as we grow the newest variety or try out the latest trend in cooking.

Having raised herbs for many years and from coast to coast, I've found them easy to grow with few pests. Most need full sun but flourish in containers and a wide range of well-drained soils, especially if enriched with compost. Following are descriptions of how to grow and use fifty-one herbs. The last chapter gives information on preserving them. Experiment and enjoy!

An exuberant mélange of herbs and flowers is part of a hundred-year-old family farm.

Herbs from the Garden

Angelica

Angelica archangelica

The licorice-like scent and flavor of angelica tend to offset the tartness of fruits such as currants, plums, gooseberries, and rhubarb. Add minced leaves or seeds to fruit compotes, pies, jellies, and jams. Simmer and steep stems and leaves with water and sugar or honey and use the syrup with desserts or dilute with water for a drink. Add to liqueurs, spirits, and wines for its flavor and digestive properties or candy the stems to flavor desserts. Add leaves to salads and use with fish, poultry, and pork, pumpkin, squash, and sweet potatoes. Stems and roots are cooked as vegetables.

How to grow. Biennial or perennial hardy to -40° F (-40° C); sun to light shade; celery-like leaves on stems 4 to 8 feet (1.2 to 2.4 m) tall; globes of tiny white flowers; mulch to keep soil cool; remove flower heads to encourage leafy growth or allow a plant to flower and reseed. Except for candied stems, plant parts are best used fresh, harvested as needed; for seeds, cut off flower heads when seeds turn pale brown.

Anise

Pimpinella anisum

Freshly minced anise leaves, with a refined licorice flavor, enhance dips and spreads made from bland cheeses, work magic garnishing soups or vegetables, or complement mixed green salads.

Use anise seeds, whole or ground, in breads and crackers; pastries, cakes, cookies, and fruit desserts; soup stock, soups; and stews; egg and cheese dishes; and with salad greens.

Tall and majestic, angelica is striking in the garden.

It is also used as a digestive in many liqueurs, including French *pastis* and Greek *ouzo*. Anisette is a combination of anise, coriander, and fennel seeds in sweetened vodka.

How to grow. Annual; full sun; bright green, feathery leaves on floppy stalks to 2 feet (61 cm) tall; flat clusters of tiny yellow-white flowers. Harvest leaves any time and use fresh or dried. Cut off seed heads when brown but before they open.

Anise Hyssop

Agastache foeniculum

Botanically allied to hyssop, anise hyssop has leaves and flowers that lean toward the licorice flavor of anise. Native to North America and used by the Great Plains Indians as a sweetener and medicine, the violet-blue flowers and leaves of anise hyssop are used mainly in beverages, cakes, cookies, and fruit dishes; with vegetables like squash, sweet potatoes, and carrots; or with sweet-and-sour main courses. The dried flowers and leaves give scent and color to potpourris and dried arrangements.

How to grow. Perennial hardy to -40° F (-40° C); full sun; bushy plants to 3 feet (91 cm) tall; flowers in late summer and fall. Use leaves or flowers fresh or dried.

Arugula

Eruca vesicaria **subsp.** *sativa*

With a flavor variously described as pungent, piquant, bitter, nutty, and peppery mustard, arugula is an acquired taste that has finally caught on with Americans. It is used mainly as a salad green but also contributes a freshness to omelets, soups, stir-fries, sauces, and sautéed vegetables. Fresh citrus, olives, artichoke hearts, and roasted peppers are complemented by it, as are goat, feta, and blue cheeses.

Also called rocket, roquette, rugula, and rucola, arugula has rosettes of wavy-edged leaves that resemble those of radishes or oakleaf lettuce. A rich source of iron and vitamins A and C, arugula is easily grown during the cooler months of the growing season. When the plants start to bloom during hot weather, enjoy the edible flowers. Leaves are used only fresh and are best harvested when young before the central stem starts to grow.

How to grow. Annual; full sun to light shade; stems grow 2 feet (61 cm) tall. Make successive plantings every two weeks in spring and late summer.

Basil

Ocimum spp.

The richly spicy flavor of basil has overtones of clove, mint, and pepper and complements a host of foods. Add fresh leaves to soup stocks or poaching liquids. Pair with lemon, garlic, thyme, and marjoram. Toss whole leaves and flowers with salads or use as a garnish. Flavor vinegars or oils with basil.

There are over twenty types of basils, with scents or tastes ranging from lemon, anise, cinnamon, cloves, or camphor. 'Thyrsiflora', or Thai, basil has a very sweet fragrance and flavor. Leaf sizes extend from the 1/4-inch-wide (60-mm-wide) foliage of 'Nano Compatto Vero' to the 3-inch (7.5-cm) or larger leaves of lettuce-leaf basil. 'Dark Opal' and 'Purple Ruffles' basils have maroon to purple leaves.

How to grow. Annual; full sun; size ranges from 6 inches (15 cm) to 6 feet (1.8 m); pinch growth to encourage branching. Harvest as needed; use fresh or preserve by blending with oil, vinegar, or water and freezing.

Bay

Laurus nobilis

The herb of champions, bay (or laurel) is added almost as a reflex action to soups, stocks, stews, marinades, tomato sauces, pickling mixtures, shellfish boils, and any long-cooked meat dish. The deliciously warm, aromatic scent and flavor also lend themselves to grain, rice, and bean dishes and even enhance fruit punches. Bay leaves are usually added dry; if using a fresh leaf, remove it halfway through the cooking time.

How to grow. Evergreen tree hardy to 10° F (-12.3° C); can be grown indoors in winter; full sun to light shade. Press leaves flat to dry.

Bergamot, Bee Balm

Monarda didyma

Like miniature fireworks, the flowers of bergamot add sparkling taste and color to salads, hot or cold beverages, desserts,

Golden calendulas blend with creeping zinnias and sunflowers.

or whatever benefits from its citrusy flavor. Brighten up fruit punches, iced tea, or anything in need of a garnish with flowers in shades of scarlet, maroon, pink, lavender, purple, or white. Toss minced fresh leaves or flowers with yogurt, honey, and fruit for an easy, healthful dessert or snack. They complement meats like pork, sausage, duck, or goose and combine well with basil or mint. Use leaves to flavor apple, plum, or wine jellies, then add a flower to each jar.

Native to the eastern United States, bergamot or bee balm is a favorite flower garden plant, and it attracts hummingbirds. Dried leaves and flowers are added to potpourris.

How to grow. Perennial hardy to -30° F (-34.5° C); full sun to partial shade; 3 to 4 feet tall; blooms in summer; cut plants back after flowering. Use leaves and flowers fresh or dried.

Borage

Borago officinalis

The translucent blue star-shaped flowers of borage, with their cucumber flavor, are among the most favored of herbal flowers for garnishing and candying. Float them in punch bowls or iced drinks, freeze them in ice cubes, toss them with a green salad, or scatter them over sliced tomatoes and cucumbers drizzled with a borage vinaigrette.

Add some leaves to soup stock, a pot of mixed greens, or vinegar. Mix minced leaves with fresh cheese or cooked chicken and butter or mayonnaise to make a delightful spread for tea sandwiches. Borage complements light meats such as fish and poultry, cheese or egg dishes, most vegetables, and salad dressings. A tea made from borage leaves makes the perfect base for a punch or sorbet. The flavor fuses nicely with burnet, dill, and mint.

How to grow. Annual; full sun; floppy stems to 2 to 3 feet (61 to 91 cm) tall; 1-inch (2.6-cm) flowers in midsummer. Use borage leaves fresh and flowers fresh or candied.

Burnet

Poterium sanguisorba

The cucumber-like flavor of burnet leaves is a pleasant addition to mixed green salads, potato salads, coleslaws, marinated vegetables, vinaigrettes, and salad dressings in addition to herb-flavored vinegars, butters, and cheeses. Use the pink flowers in salads and tea sandwiches and as a garnish. Add both the leaves and the flowers to iced drinks.

How to grow. Perennial hardy to -40° F (-40° C); full sun to light shade; fern-like leaves in open rosettes to 1 foot(30.5 cm) tall; 1-inch (2.6 cm) rounded clusters of tiny flowers. Use burnet leaves and flowers fresh, frozen, or to flavor vinegar. Harvest at any time.

Calendula

Calendula officinalis

The calendula marigold (not to be confused with American marigolds, which are not used as culinary herbs) has an herbal history going back to the Romans and was very popular in the Elizabethan era. Fresh or dried petals add their golden color and green, peppery flavor to soups, stews, eggs, salads, sandwiches, cheese, butter, grains, wine, dumplings, cakes, and puddings.

Sometimes called poor man's saffron, the daisy-like flowers of calendula are more than a substitute. The best calendulas for eating are the species and the varieties with large petals like 'Pacific Beauty', 'Indian Prince', and 'Sunglow'.

How to grow. Annual; full sun; 8 to 24 inches (20 to 61 cm) tall; yellow, orange, and apricot daisy-like flowers close at night and in rainy weather; grow a pot indoors in winter in a bright, cool room. Fresh or dried, use small whole flowers or with the petals separated.

Caraway

Carum carvi

Synonymous with rye bread, caraway is an ancient herb used by many cultures for more than 5,000 years. Besides in breads, most people think of using the seeds with cakes, cookies, beef stews, pork, and cabbage, but caraway also harmonizes with other vegetables, eggs, cheese, soups, and stews. Apples and caraway seeds are a good match; add the seeds to apples sauced, baked, fried, stewed, or made into pies. Nibble the digestive seeds after dinner, either plain or candied, or sip a homemade version of Kümmel or aquavit.

The young leaves are also delightful in salads, of either mixed greens or fruit, and in soups and herb cheeses and butters. The root, too, can be eaten; it resembles that of a carrot, to which it is related.

How to grow. Biennial hardy to -40° F (-40° C); full sun; feathery foliage on floppy stems to 2 feet (61 cm) tall; flat white flower clusters. Harvest fresh foliage as needed; gather seed heads when ripe; harvest roots after gathering seeds and use fresh.

Chervil

Anthriscus cerefolium

Subtle and warm, the taste of chervil commingles parsley, myrrh, and anise. Chervil's refreshing flavor and sweet aroma complements beets, carrots, corn, spinach, sorrel, peas, green beans, fish, eggs, and cheese. Traditionally combined with parsley, chives, and tarragon in the French *fines herbes*, chervil also is added to classic bearnaise and bechamel sauces as well as vinaigrettes. Let chervil lend its essence to a clear broth plus sorrel or spinach soups. Add the lacy leaves to green salads or use as a garnish.

However you use it, add chervil at the end of cooking, as long heating causes the flavor to turn harsh. Use it fresh, to flavor oil, or mixed with butter and frozen. Chervil is most flavorful during cool weather and just prior to blooming.

How to grow. Annual; best in cool, moist weather; light shade; plain or curly leaves, 1 to 2 feet (30.5 to 61 cm) tall; clusters of small white flowers; pinch out emerging flower stalks to prolong growth; allow a few plants to go to seed or make successive sowings; grow in cold frame, greenhouse, or indoors in winter.

Chives

Allium schoenoprasum

When in full bloom with its starburst globes of mauve, no garden flower is more spectacular than chives. Used for more than 5,000 years and encountered by Marco Polo in his travels to China, chives have a delicate, onion-like flavor that complements just about any vegetable, poultry, seafood, cheese, or egg dish. Stir in just before serving sauces, soups, or stews, sprinkle over food as a garnish, or make chive butter or cream cheese. Whole chive stems make perfect decorative ribbons for tying around bundles of beans, carrot matchsticks, or spears of asparagus. Chives are also an element in the French *fines herbes*. Stems and flowers can be tossed in salads. Use the flowers to flavor and color vinegar.

Minced chives can be dried or frozen, but they will lose much of their flavor. Pot up a clump in the fall, let it lie dormant outside for several months, then bring it indoors during the rest of winter, or use 'Grolou', the best variety for growing indoors.

How to grow. Bulbs hardy to -40° F (-40° C); full sun; slender hollow leaves 18 to 24 inches (45 to 61 cm) tall. Harvest leaves close to the ground.

Coriander, Cilantro

Coriandrum sativum

The scent of fresh coriander, usually referred to as cilantro, is likened to that of bedbugs, with the common name coming from the Greek word for same. One of the bitter herbs mentioned in the Bible for Passover, it was also used in the ancient civilizations of China, Rome, and Egypt. Today it figures in cuisines around the globe.

Use the fresh parlsey-like leaves or roots with salads, marinades, salsas, stews, stir-fries, rice, pasta, or shellfish. An uncooked sauce of finely minced coriander leaves, garlic, ginger, green chili, with perhaps some lemon juice and mint, is pefect with curries. Dried and used whole or ground, coriander seeds add a warm taste to curry powders, marinades, salad dressings, pickles, eggs, cheese, lamb, sausage, chutneys, cooked fruit, breads, cookies, and cakes. A few crushed seeds also add a distinctive note to a cup of coffee.

How to grow. Annual; full sun or light shade; floppy stems 24 to 30 inches (61 to 76 cm) tall; white flowers; make succession plantings every two to three weeks or choose varieties slow to mature; allow a few plants to go to seed. Harvest leaves and roots as needed; gather seed heads as the scent changes from that of bedbugs to that of oranges.

Cumin

Cuminum cyminum

Indispensable to curry powder, a pot of *frijoles*, chili, sausage, or other dishes of Mexican, North African, Indian, or Portuguese origin, cumin is difficult to grow as it needs a long, hot summer for seeds to mature. An ancient herb of the Mediterranean, cumin seed has a distinctive, dominant, peppery flavor.

Use it in casseroles, lentil soup, pilafs, or chutneys or with potatoes or couscous. The leaves are not used in cooking.

How to grow. Annual; full sun; finely cut leaves and sprawling stems to 12 inches (30.5 cm); small clusters of pink-white flowers. Harvest seeds when ripe three to four months after sowing.

Dill

Anethum graveolens

Synonymous with pickles, dill has a unique tangy-sweet flavor that wends its way through other foods via feathery blue-green leaves and flattened elliptical seeds. Egg and cheese dishes, soups, salads, dips, butters, and sauces are complemented by dill, as are meats ranging from fish to lamb, poultry, and pork. Many vegetables also go well with it, but especially cucumbers, asparagus, spinach, sauerkraut, and potatoes. Dill vinegar is made by steeping green seed heads in a pint of white wine vinegar.

How to grow. Annual; full sun; single hollow stems to 3 feet (91 cm) tall; flat clusters of yellow flowers. 'Tetra', 'Dukat', and 'Bouquet' are shorter, produce lots of leaves, and are slow to flower; 'Fernleaf' grows 18 inches (45 cm) tall with multi-branching stems. Make successive plantings every three weeks; let some plants self-sow. Do not plant dill and fennel close together as they cross-pollinate. Best leaf flavor is just before the flowers open; use fresh or frozen; harvest seeds as they turn brown.

Fennel

Foeniculum vulgare

Resembling dill in appearance and anise in flavor, fennel is inextricably linked with fish, whether as part of a poaching stock, sauce, mayonnaise, or stuffing or with stems tossed on the grill to impart flavor as they burn. Fennel is also used with lamb, pork, and duck; in marinades, soups, vinaigrettes, salads, sausages, herb butters, beverages, and desserts; and with grains, beets, cabbage, potatoes, eggs, and cheese. In India fennel seeds are often offered at meal's end for nibbling as a digestive and breath sweetener.

Both the feathery blue-green or bronze leaves and seeds are used for flavoring. Cook the stems as a vegetable, like Florence or bulb fennel, a close relative. To maintain fennel's delicate essence, add the leaves near the end of cooking.

How to grow. Perennial grown as an annual where colder than -10° F (-23.4° C); full sun; 3 to 5 feet (91 to 152 cm) tall; flat clusters of tiny yellow flowers; make succession plantings and remove flower buds to extend leaf growth; let some plants go to seed; do not plant near dill as they cross-pollinate. Harvest seed heads as they ripen and turn brown.

Garlic

Allium sativum

Strongly scented, magical, and medicinal, garlic is an indispensable seasoning with its hot, onion-like quality. In the garden, garlic is grown as a companion plant and used in sprays for pests. For the cook, garlic is found in virtually every part of the meal save dessert, and some have even found ways to use it there. Garlic is at its mellowest when cooked slowly in stews or roasted in the oven. Burned garlic becomes bitter. To peel the cloves easily, smash them first with the flat side of a knife.

How to grow. Perennial bulb hardy to -40° F (-40° C); full sun; long thin leaves to 2 feet (61 cm) tall; plant in early fall for harvest the following summer when leaves die back.

The sweet perfume of lavender flowers
scents the air on a summer day.

Lemon balm combines the refreshing scent and flavor
of citrus with a touch of mint.

Garlic Chives

Allium tuberosum

One of the most versatile of herbs in the garden, garlic chives hold their own in the kitchen with the subtle garlic flavor of their flat leaves and the honey-and-garlic quality of their white flower clusters. Use fresh minced leaves with whatever might benefit from their mild quality, be it soups, stews, or salads and chicken, pork, lamb, beef, or fish, adding them near the end of cooking or just before serving. Toss the flowers into salads, add to cooked vegetables, butters, dips, sauces, or stir-fries, or use as a garnish.

How to grow. Perennial hardy to -40° F (-40° C); full sun; flat, thin leaves to 18 inches (45 cm) tall; globes of long-lasting white flowers; readily self-sows. Use leaves fresh or frozen; use flowers fresh or to flavor vinegar.

Ginger

Zingiber officinale

What would life be without gingerbread men and ginger ale? Soothing to the digestion and stimulating to the circulation, the finger-like smooth-skinned rhizomatous roots of ginger reveal a pale golden interior when peeled. Fresh ginger is essential to stir-fried dishes and curries. Store fresh ginger, peeled and cut into chunks, in a bottle of vodka or sherry kept in the refrigerator. Dried and powdered, ginger is used in cakes, cookies, and desserts as well as pickles, chutneys, and preserves.

How to grow. Perennial hardy to 20° F (-6.7° C); light shade outdoors; bright light indoors; 2 to 4 feet (61 to 122 cm) tall; grow in 12-inch (30.5-cm) pots and winter indoors in cold regions.

Horseradish

Armoracia rusticana

Not just for roast beef, horseradish has an acrid quality reminiscent of mustard and counterpoints fresh and smoked fish, tongue, sausages, chicken, eggs, asparagus, avocado, beets, carrots, potatoes, turnips, and coleslaw. Freshly grated root is variously mixed with vinegar, mayonnaise, cream, sour cream, butter, or yogurt to serve with foods. Cooking destroys the pungency, as does sitting around in a refrigerator after grating unless covered with vinegar. It's best to grate a bit of the fresh white root as needed. Add a 2-inch (5-cm) piece to each quart of low-salt pickles to keep them crisp. Combined with grated apple, it provides a classic condiment for fish or meat.

The young, tender leaves can be added to mixed green salads, and the root is a rich source of vitamin C and has antibiotic qualities.

12

How to grow. Perennial hardy to -20° F (-28.9° C); full sun; long, strap-like leaves 1 to 2 feet (30.5 to 61 cm) long; 2- to 3-foot (61- to 91-cm) spikes of tiny edible white flowers; growth can be invasive. Harvest one- or two-year-old roots in late fall; scrub and dry the roots, then store them in the crisper drawer of the refrigerator or pack in dry sand set in a cool, dark place.

Hyssop

Hyssopus officinalis

Butterflies flock to hyssop's spikes of tiny blue, pink, or white flowers all summer long, and bees make a wonderful honey feasting on the nectar. The minty, camphor-like scent and warm, spicy flavor of the leaves intrigue as well. Use hyssop as you would thyme or savory, adding it to soups, stews, sausages, meats, or fish. Toss young leaves and flowers in with salads or use with fruits, especially peaches, pears, apricots, plums, figs, or cranberries.

How to grow. Semi-evergreen woody shrub hardy to -30° F (-34.5° C); full sun or light shade; many-stemmed clumps to 2 feet (61 cm) tall; prune back in spring and again after flowering to encourage growth. Use leaves and flowers fresh or dried.

Lavender

Lavandula spp.

With its singular sweet scent, lavender is first thought of for the linen closet, the bath, or the medicine cabinet, but the perfumed presence of the flowers can also be found in vinegars, cakes, cookies, pies, puddings, fruit desserts, jellies, and beverages. Lavender varieties have stalks of tiny lilac, purple, pink, or white flowers.

Forming bushy plants with narrow blue-grey leaves, lavender is a wonderful ornamental plant, especially when planted in masses or as an edging for beds of herbs or old roses. Noted varieties of hardy true lavender (*Lavandula angustifolia*) include 'Grey Lady', which has very grey leaves and is particularly hardy; 'Hidcote', with deep purple flowers; 'Munstead', with short growth and early blooms; and 'Twickel' with deep lavender-blue flowers and very grey leaves. There are a number of other lavenders that can also be grown as houseplants.

How to grow. *Lavandula angustifolia* cultivars are woody shrubs hardy to -20° F (-28.9° C) and colder with protection; full sun; soil must be light, well-drained, and neutral to alkaline; 18 to 30 inches (45 to 76 cm) tall. Harvest flowers just as they begin to open or when fully opened; use fresh or dried.

Lemon Balm

Melissa officinalis

Lemon balm is an easily grown, soothing herb with an intense yet delicate lemon flavor and scent underpinned with mint. Although the flavor is best when fresh, dried leaves are used for tea and potpourri. Minced fresh leaves readily substitute for lemon zest. Often added to beverages–hot or iced tea, fruit juices, wine punches–lemon balm also contributes to salads, salad dressings, marinades, eggs, fish, lamb, poultry, soups, stews, sauces, fruits, jams, jellies, and even milk dishes such as custard.

How to grow. Perennial hardy to -30° F (-34.5° C); full sun to light shade; loose shrub to 3 feet (91 cm) tall with bright green, scallop-edged leaves; there is a variegated variety. Harvest leaves anytime to use fresh; to dry, harvest leaves before plant flowers by cutting plants off 2 inches above the ground.

Lemongrass

Cymbopogon citratus

Strongly lemon scented and long savored for its sour-lemon taste in tropical Southeast Asian countries where it is native, lemongrass has begun to be used widely in the United States only in the last several decades. Add the tender inner stalks to traditional Thai and Vietnamese dishes and curries, but also experiment by adding it to marinades, soups, sauces, beverages, or any food lemon enhances. Tea brewed from it is high in vitamin A.

How to grow. Perennial hardy to 30° F (-1.2° C); in colder areas, grow as a potted plant, summering it outdoors; full sun. Harvest by removing stem at base, cutting off upper leaves, peeling tough outer leaves, and using the tender inner stalk; use fresh, dried, or frozen.

Lemon Verbena

Aloysia triphylla

An herb native to Argentina and Chile, lemon verbena is stronger flavored than the other lemon herbs and is used in smaller amounts. When fresh, the leaves may be steeped whole in marinades, salad dressings, and beverages, then removed before serving. When dried, they easily crumble and readily flavor fish, poultry, muffins, sweet breads, jellies, jams, desserts, and beverages. The flavor is good anytime, but best just before the small white flower clusters open.

How to grow. Deciduous woody shrub hardy to 15° F (-9.5° C); in colder areas, grow as a potted plant, summering it outdoors, or grow as an annual; full sun; 5 to 15 feet (1.5 to 4.5 m) tall; pinch growth to keep plants bushy. Harvest and use fresh leaves as desired or dry leaves for winter use.

Lovage

Levisticum officinale

Use celery-like flavored leaves and stems fresh in salads and fresh, dried, or frozen as part of a bouquet garni in soups, stews, or sauces or cooked with vegetables, grains, quiches, beef, lamb, pork, or poultry. Candy or blanch the fresh stems as a vegetable. Seeds, whole or ground, substitute for celery seed in pickles, breads, and cookies. Dried and freshly ground, all parts give no-salt herb seasonings substance.

How to grow. Perennial hardy to -40° F (-40° C); full sun to light shade; long, ribbed, hollow stems to 4 feet (1.5 m) tall; glossy, dark green divided leaves; clusters of tiny yellow flowers; remove flower buds to force bushy growth. Young leaves and stems have the best flavor. To freeze, puree with half as much water as lovage and freeze in ice cube tray, storing cubes in plastic freezer bags. Harvest seed heads when brown.

Marjoram

Origanum majorana

Naturally blending with other staples of the herb garden, such as bay, thyme, garlic, and basil, marjoram is a sweeter, gentler kin of oregano. Use it to flavor oils and vinegars as well as soups, stews, stuffings, and marinades. Add near the end of cooking.

How to grow. Perennial hardy to 20° F (-6.7° C); often grown as an annual; full sun; open, bushy plant 12 to 18 inches (30.5 to 45 cm) tall with small oval, grey-green, fuzzy leaves; knot-like buds open to tiny white or pink flowers. Harvest fresh leaves as needed. For the biggest yield of leaves to dry, pinch out flower buds, then harvest when plants again have flower buds, cutting to the ground.

Mexican Marigold Mint

Tagetes lucida

Known by several common names, Mexican marigold mint grows indigenously throughout Mexico and Guatemala. Its flavor strongly resembles that of anise or tarragon, but unlike them, it grows readily in hot, dry climates. Use with salads, cheese, fish, poultry, sauces, pickles, and vinegar. It blends especially well with orange or tomato. Add to hot and cold beverages, including sangria and wine punches, plus mulled cider or wine. Brighten salads or pastas with the edible flowers.

How to grow. Perennial hardy to 0° F (-17.8° C); full sun; bushy plants 24 inches (61 cm) tall; narrow glossy green leaves; clusters of 1-inch (2.5-cm) yellow flowers; grow indoors in winter; can become invasive from self-sowing. Best used fresh; use dried in tea or potpourri.

Mint

Mentha spp.

Cool and refreshing, mint's fragrance and flavor permeate our culture from candy to juleps, iced tea, jelly, sauces, tabbouleh, chewing gum, mouthwash, toothpaste, and cigarettes. Mints are a profligate lot, with some twenty-five species producing more than six hundred named cultivars.

A symbol of hospitality, mint has flavors and scents that run the gamut from apple, chocolate, and grapefruit, to lime, orange, or pineapple. Most varieties have plain, pointed leaves, but some have variegated foliage.

Peppermint has a stronger flavor and is used mainly for hot or cold tea. The best-flavored variety is 'Blue Balsam'. Ground-hugging Corsican mint (*M. Requienii*) is intensely flavored, too. Spearmint is the culinary hero of the family, with 'Kentucky Colonel' having

an especially rich flavor and aroma. It can be used with dried beans and grains, meats, fish, vegetables, and fruits and pairs naturally with chocolate.

How to grow. Perennial hardy to -20° F (-28.9° C); full sun to light shade; varieties vary from less than an inch (2.5 cm) to 2 feet (61 cm) or more; toothed leaves in opposite pairs on square stems; spikes of tiny purple, pink, or white flower. To keep from being invasive, plant in sunken flue tiles or bottomless cans set at least 10 inches (25 cm) deep or grow in containers. Use fresh, dried, or frozen, or overwinter in a pot indoors.

Mustard

Brassica spp.

This golden condiment is the crowning touch to sandwiches, vinaigrettes, or roasted meat. Sharp, acrid herbs, clearing sinuses and relieving rheumatism, the mustards composing commerical preparations are white mustard (*B. hirta*), which is usually called yellow mustard seed in cookbooks, brown mustard (*B. juncea*), and occasionally black mustard (*B. nigra*). Ballpark mustards are mainly from white seeds; English and German mustards are blends of white and brown; Oriental and Dijon mustard rely more on brown mustard, which also produces the mustard greens beloved in the South.

Whole seeds are often added to pickled vegetables, fruits, and meats; whole or ground seeds or prepared mustards are used in sauces, salad dressings, and as a seasoning for meats and vegetables. Add the edible flowers to salads.

How to grow. Annual; plant in early spring or early fall; full sun; grows to 4 feet (1.2 m) tall; yellow flowers. Harvest the seed pods when they turn brown but before they split open.

Nasturtium

Tropaeolum majus

Peppery leaves with the flavor of watercress, spicy yet honey-sweet edible flowers in sunshine hues, and seeds mimicking capers make nasturtiums a culinary *tour de force*. Nasturtium flowers and leaves benefit salads, pastas, dips, sandwiches, and spreads with their pungency and vitamin C. No garnish is better than the yellow, gold, apricot, orange, scarlet, or mahogany 2-inch (5-cm) flowers, which are also enjoyed with a stuffing made from cheese or seafood, chicken, or tofu salad.

Versatile in the garden, the compact types, such as 'Whirlybird' or 'Jewel', fill or edge beds and flourish in containers. 'Alaska' is a compact nasturtium with variegated leaves. 'Gleam' has trailing stems that can be trained to trellises.

How to grow. Annual; full sun; 6 inches (15 cm) to 6 feet (3.7 m); with too much fertilizer plants produce more leaves than flowers. Use leaves and flowers fresh. Pickle the seeds while still green.

Oregano

Origanum spp.

Likened to a hotter, spicier marjoram, oregano obviously goes with tomatoes, cheese, and beans, but also egg and cheese combinations, eggplant, zucchini, roasted peppers, fish and shellfish stews, and grilled, roasted, or stewed meats. Because of its pungency, it can be used with long, slow cooking, and its flavor is as emphatic dried as fresh.

Getting an oregano with a sufficiently strong flavor and winter hardiness requires perseverance and blind luck. Try to taste-test a leaf, or else trust the description in the mail-order herb catalog. The flavor of oregano can vary among climates, soils, and years.

Generally, wild oregano (*O. vulgare*)

is not as flavorful as plants labeled Greek oregano, winter marjoram, winter sweet marjoram, or pot marjoram, any of which may be listed as *O. heracleoticum*, *O. vulgare* subsp. *hirtum*, *O. hirtum*, or *O. vulgare* 'Olympicum'. Some sources list *O. vulgare* var. *prismaticum* or their own selection as having the best flavor. Be willing to take chances.

Indoor alternatives are the tender perennials Mexican oregano (*Lippia graveolens*) and Mt. Pima oregano (*Monarda austromontana*).

How to grow. Perennial hardy to -20° F (-28.9° C); full sun; bushy, spreading plant 1 to 2 feet (30.5 to 61 cm) tall; small oval leaves; small purple or white edible flowers. To harvest for drying, trim plants back close to the ground in early summer and again in two months.

Parsley

Petroselinum crispum

Parsley is like a good friend we take for granted; remove it from foods and they would not be the same. Its fresh "green" taste brightens and blends the flavors surrounding it, and it is also a significant source of vitamins A, B, and especially C, plus minerals, most notably iron.

Parsley grows in three forms: curly parsley (*P. crispum* var. *crispum*) has finely divided and twisted leaves; flat-leaf, or Italian, parsley (*P. crispum* var. *neapolitanum*), has the strongest flavor and is generally preferred for flavoring; Hamburg parsley (*P. crispum* var. *tuberosum*) has both flat leaves and edible white roots. Grow at least six to have plenty for harvesting, picking the outermost leaves.

Of the curly type, 'Forest Green' is recommended for its ability to stay green well into winter and 'Krausa' for its flavor. For flat-leaf parsley, 'Gigante d'Italia' (Giant Italian) has the sweetest flavor.

How to grow. Biennial hardy to -10° F (-23.4° C); full sun to light shade; 12 to 24 inches (30.5 to 61 cm) tall; will stay green all winter in a cold frame; can be grown in a pot indoors.

Peppers

Capsicum spp.

Life would be bland without the dozens of chili pepper varieties that flavor salsa, chile con carne, barbecue, jambalaya, sambal, satay, tandoori chicken, and curry. Even for those who don't like hot food, a small amount of hot pepper seasoning enhances other flavors.

For all the diversity of shape, color, and size of hot and sweet bell peppers, they all come under the classification of *C. annuum* var. *annuum* except for tabasco peppers, which are *C. frutescens*. Hot peppers are hot because of capsaicin, an almost indestructible alkaloid concentrated in the veins near the seeds of the pepper. Capsaicin increases blood circulation and facilitates perspiration. It can also irritate the eyes, so wear gloves when handling hot peppers and remove them immediately when done. High in vitamins A and C, plus minerals, hot peppers are recommended by herbalists for a variety of internal and external applications.

Numerous hot peppers are available in the American Southwest. The five most common, in ascending order of heat, are Anaheim (also called green or California), poblano (called ancho when dried), cayenne, jalapeño, and serrano.

How to grow. Perennial grown as annual; full sun; 12 to 36 inches (30.5 to 91 cm) tall. Harvest and use fresh at either the green or ripened red stage. Thick-fleshed hot peppers like Anaheims and jalapeños can be preserved by canning, and thin-walled ones like poblanos, cayennes, and serranos dry readily.

Poppy

Papaver spp.

The sweet nutty flavor and crunchy texture of tiny poppy seeds enriches cakes, pastries, strudels, breads, salad dressings, noodles, and dumplings, as well as other dishes of Middle Eastern and Indian origin. A large family of plants, poppies have single or double intensely colored flowers with translucent petals in shades of red, orange, yellow, apricot, pink, or lavender. All varieties produce edible seeds in globe-shaped pods of ornamental value when dried. Most of the commercially available poppy seed is from the red poppy (*P. rhoeas*) or the opium poppy (*P. somniferum*), with the seed containing none of the narcotic property.

How to grow. Red and opium poppies are annual; full sun; 18 to 36 inches (45 to 91 cm) tall; jagged edged, grey-green leaves. Although seed can be purchased for opium poppies, it is illegal to grow them in most places. Harvest the pods when they turn brown and are dry.

Rose

Rosa spp.

Rose petals can appear in salads, sauces, fish or poultry dishes, vinegars, crepes, cookies, cakes, puddings, ice creams, sorbets, and jellies. Whole flowers are used as a garnish or candied, while rose water flavors desserts.

Any fragrant rose grown without harmful pesticides can be used in cooking, with red or dark pink the preferred color. Best known of the old roses are the apothecary's rose (*R. gallica* var. *officinalis*), cabbage roses (*R. centifolia*), and damask roses (*R. damascena*). These bloom only once each year, so other fragrant, red or pink repeat-blooming old roses are also grown for cooking, such as 'Madame Isaac Pereire', 'Zephirine Drouhin', 'Rose du Roi', 'Grüss an Teplitz', 'Henry Nevard', and 'Rose de Rescht'. Easiest to grow, most hardy, and usually very fragrant are the rugosas. Best for candying are modern miniature roses.

How to grow. Woody shrubs hardy to -10° F (-23.4° C) or colder with protection; rugosas are hardy to -50° F (-45.6° C); full sun; 3 to 6 feet (91 to 183 cm) tall; miniatures 1 foot (30.5 cm) tall. Use fresh or preserve by candying small whole flowers or separating petals and drying. Purchase rose water at health food or gourmet stores.

Rose Geranium

Pelargonium spp.

From the more than 200 varieties of scented geraniums, bearing fragrances such as apple, coconut, lime, lemon, nutmeg, and peppermint, the rose geranium is most popular in the kitchen, scenting cakes, cookies, custards, puddings, jams, jellies, ice creams, wine and fruit punches, vinegars, teas, lemonades, and fruits.

Rose geraniums are a kin of the tender garden geraniums we rely on for bright summer color, as opposed to the hardy perennial true geraniums. There are a number of cultivars, including ones with lemon or mint undertones, and different leaf shapes, plant sizes, or flower colors. The rose fragrance can vary with the time of day, time of year, soil, and climate, so one can only scratch-and-sniff if buying locally or order blindly and hope.

How to grow. Perennial grown as an annual or overwintered indoors; full sun; 2 to 3 feet (61 to 91 cm) tall; velvety divided leaves on branching, shrubby plants; edible flowers are pink, white, or red. Use leaves fresh or preserve by layering with sugar or drying.

Rosemary

Rosmarinus officinalis

Possessed of a resinous quality with a bit of lemon, mint, and ginger as well, rosemary was for centuries primarily a medicinal and cosmetic herb, and many aromatherapy preparations today rely on its volatile oil. In the kitchen, rosemary, fresh or dried, synthesizes with beef, pork, poultry, lamb, venison, salmon, tuna, halibut, eggs, and cheese. Partner it with potatoes, tomatoes, squash, greens, peas, eggplant, mushrooms, beans, and lentils. Rosemary adds substance to soups, dumplings, rice, sauces, salad dressings, vinegars, oils, marinades, and butters. Neither are the sweets left out: cook rosemary with fruits and add to jelly and honey. Include some in biscuits, breads, and wine or fruit drinks. Edible, the flowers make lovely garnishes or gently flavor foods when added near the end of cooking. Be sure to toss some rosemary onto the fire during the last 5 or 10 minutes of grilling.

Over a dozen cultivars of rosemary provide a range of flower colors, including shades of blue from pale to dark, white, and pink. Most grow into small woody shrubs, but others creep along the ground or cascade over walls.

How to grow. Evergreen shrub hardy to 10° F (-12.3° C), except 'Arp', which is hardy to -10° F (-23.4° C); full sun; 3 to 6 feet (91 to 183 cm) tall; small grey-green, needle-like leaves; 1/2-inch (1-cm) flowers. Use fresh or dried.

Saffron

Crocus sativus

Saffron is the world's most expensive herb; anywhere from 50,000 to 250,000 crocuses are needed to make a pound of saffron. A fall-blooming form of spring's diminutive harbinger, saffron crocus has long been used as a medicinal and culinary herb.

Fortunately only a small pinch is necessary to impart its golden color, fragrance, and bittersweet flavor to such traditional dishes as bouillabaise, risotto, and paella, in addition to cakes, cookies, and breads. Use it, too, with fresh cheeses, eggs, lamb, poultry, and pork, with garlic, fish, and shellfish being its best partners.

How to grow. Bulb hardy to -10° F (-23.4° C); full sun to light shade; narrow, grass-like leaves 4 to 6 inches (10 to 15 cm) tall; purple flowers. Harvest the bright orange stigmas just as the flowers open. Use fresh or dried, moistening the dried ones in water before using in food.

Sage

Salvia officinalis

Variously described as having a balsam or camphor taste, sage is an herb of intensity with a mellow flavor when used fresh. Flavor can vary among plants, sites, and seasons. Cooks of Italian origin or influence know that sage goes well with liver, veal, and sausages. Use it with meat or strong-flavored fish when grilling or include it in grain-and-herb or green salads. Eggs, cheese, cream soups, chowders, stews, roasts, poultry, rabbit, pork, and venison as well as most vegetables, especially potatoes, go well with sage. Add to breads and fruit and wine drinks or brew it into tea, hot or cold. Sage honey is a delicacy.

Of the over seven hundred and fifty species of sage, one stands out in the kitchen. There are several cultivars with distinctive foliage, including green-and-gold variegated leaves, purple foliage, and leaves variegated with cream, purple, and green. Some people substitute Cleveland sage (*S. Clevelandii*) for garden sage. Pineapple sage (*S. elegans*), fruit-flavored sage (*S. Dorisiana*), and 'Honeydew Melon' sage have appropriately scented leaves and bright scarlet flowers. These have limited uses in beverages, jellies, and desserts and with chicken and cheese.

How to grow. Woody shrub hardy to -20° F (-28.9° C); full sun; 12 to 30 inches (30.5 to 76 cm) tall; rough-textured, 2-inch grey-green leaves; stalks of purple flowers; prune back by half in spring; grow fruit sages as annuals. Use fresh or dried.

Savory

Satureja spp.

Associated with satyrs and satisfaction by the Romans, savory was given its common name in deference to its flavor. Complementary to all types of beans, savory is also exemplary in no-salt herb blends, with salads, cheese, vegetables, and white wine, and for reducing the cooking odors of cabbage family members. With a sharp, slightly bitter, pepper-like flavor, savory melds with pork, sausage, poultry, and fish, whether stewed, roasted, marinated, grilled, or baked, especially when combined with other Mediterranean herbs. Flavor vinegar with savory or plant it close to beehives for exceptional honey.

Summer savory (*S. hortensis*) is an annual growing to 18 inches (45 cm) tall with narrow, grey-green, tender 1-inch (2.5-cm) leaves. White or pale pink flowers adorn the stems throughout summer and fall.

A semievergreen perennial, winter savory (*S. montana*) grows slightly shorter, with smaller, tougher, darker green leaves and lilac-pink flowers. Creeping and trailing forms are available. It takes to pruning and is useful for edging or defining knot gardens. The flavor is stronger, and only half as much is used in cooking.

How to grow. Winter savory is a perennial hardy to -10° F (-23.4° C); full sun; both savories grow well in pots, indoors or out. To preserve summer savory, harvest as it comes into flower, cutting it off close to the ground, then drying. Where hardy, winter savory provides fresh leaves year-round.

Sesame

Sesamum indicum

Among the oldest of foods, sesame seeds are primarily used for producing a high-quality, health-promoting cooking oil that seldom turns rancid. To those who know the delight of Charleston's benne wafers, the luxury of creamy tahini in hummus or baba ghanouj, or the crunchy taste of toasted seeds in a stir-fry, sesame seeds are indispensable.

Either whole or lightly crushed, toasted sesame seeds make a good salt-free seasoning for sprinkling on salads, vegetables, chicken, turkey cutlets, or fish before baking or sautéeing. Their nutty flavor enriches breads, piecrusts, and crumb toppings, while sesame seed brittle and halvah nourish the sweet tooth. Unless they are to be browned in cooking, toast seeds before using.

How to grow. Annual; full sun; 3 feet (91 cm) tall; oval, sometimes lobed leaves 5 inches (12.5 cm) long; 1-inch (2.5-cm) pale pink or white flowers; a long, hot growing season and twenty-five plants are needed to yield 1 cup of seed. Harvest seed pods about a month after flowers open and before the capsules shatter.

Shallot

Allium cepa

Shallots combine the best qualtities of onions, garlic, green onions, and chives with their own subtleties to create a mild, flavorful entity. Some people prefer the small shallots with orange-brown skin, while others say the pungent, long grey or pink ones are better.

Be sure not to brown shallots when cooking, or they will turn bitter. Use them for flavoring sauces, fish, shellfish, poultry, stews, soups, oils, butters, vinegars, salads, salad dressings, and eggs. Shallots also pickle superbly, and the green tops are useful as green onions.

Expensive to buy, shallots are as easily grown as yellow onions. One bulblet, or clove, will yield six to ten at harvest.

How to grow. Bulbs hardy to -40° F (-40° C); full sun; hollow green leaves 1 to 2 feet (30.5 to 61 cm) tall; plant from fall to early spring, mulching in colder climates. Use anytime the clumps reach a good size or harvest for storage when the tops start to die.

Sorrel

Rumex spp.

Lemony-flavored sorrel has the advantage of a respectable vitamin A and C content, but the disadvantage of oxalic acid, which is detrimental if consumed too often. Its invasive tendencies are easily dealt with by selecting a judicious spot for planting.

The common name is derivative of an old German word for sour. A little mince of sorrel zings up any salad and makes a splendid sauce for fish. Add a bit to any cream soup or flavor eggs or breads with it. Remove the stem and tough midrib before cooking and cook only in nonstick, enamel, or stainless-steel pans.

Several different sorrels are eaten, with English, or garden, sorrel (*R. acetosa*) most widely available. French, or buckler, sorrel (*R. scutatus*) is a daintier plant and worth the search for either plants or seeds.

How to grow. Perennials hardy to -40° F (-40° C); full sun; bright green lance-shaped leaves 2 to 12 inches (5 to 30.5 cm) long. Leaves can be harvested anytime and are best used fresh, but they can be frozen.

Sweet Cicely

Myrrhis odorata

A resplendent herb of graceful form, one of the few that takes to shade, sweet cicely can be used in all its parts to gently innervate foods. It contains as much as forty percent sugar, so the anise flavor of the leaves, stems, and seeds is most appropriate in liqueurs, cookies, cakes, or other desserts. Rhubarb, plums, strawberries, blueberries, gooseberries, and currants respond to sweet cicely, alone or combined with lemon balm or mint. Mince some into salads, salad dressings, egg dishes, and vegetables, particularly broccoli, cabbage, cauliflower, potatoes, carrots, squash, and sweet potatoes. Combined with butter and lemon juice, it sauces fish or chicken breast, or use with basil, lovage, and parsley. Fresh roots can be grated into stir-fries, salads, or baked goods, boiled and eaten as a salad or side dish, or candied as a sweet.

Forming a luxurious mass of leaves resembling ferns or chervil, sweet cicely is one of the first plants up in the spring and last to go in the fall.

How to grow. Perennial hardy to -40° F (-40° C); light shade; feathery leaves 3 to 5 feet (91 to 152 cm) tall; flat clusters of small white flowers in early summer. Use all plant parts fresh; seeds may be used green or dried.

Sweet Woodruff

Galium odoratum

A calming and uplifting herb, woodruff is noted for its scent of new-mown hay mixed with vanilla, the result of coumarin in the leaves. Best known for flavoring white wine in the German May wine, where it is known as *waldmeister*, or master of the woods, woodruff is used with cognac or Benedictine by the Swiss and with champagne by the French. It also mixes well with cider and other fruit juices. Because of the coumarin content, woodruff drinks should be imbibed only occasionally.

How to grow. Perennial groundcover hardy to -40° F (-40° C); shade; whorls of narrow, dark green, pointed leaves on stems 12 inches (30.5 cm) tall; small white star-shaped flowers in spring. Use fresh or dried.

Tarragon

Artemisia dracunculus

Native to southern Europe, Asia, and the eastern United States, tarragon has a flavor and aroma of delicate, mild anise. Used since ancient civilizations, its common and scientific names come from early names meaning dragon, perhaps for its biting, numbing flavor or serpentine roots.

The flavorful French tarragon is sterile, so it cannot be reproduced from seed, only from division or cuttings. Lesser-flavored but more vigorously growing Russian or Siberian tarragons are seed-produced and sold but should be avoided. Take care to make sure you're getting the correct plant.

Thomas Jefferson shared plants among his compatriots and, no doubt, enjoyed tarragon in its traditional role with cream sauces, vinegar, fish, and shellfish. Use fresh with salads and most vegetable, meat, grain, egg, or cheese dishes. The French *fines herbes* combine tarragon with chervil, chives, and parsley. Use minced tarragon with tarragon vinegar in mayonnaises, vinaigrettes, and mustards. Because it gets bitter with long cooking, add to slow-cooked soups and stews during the last 15 minutes.

How to grow. Perennial hardy to -20° F (-28.9° C); full sun; floppy stems to 2 feet (61 cm) tall with small, narrow leaves 1 to 3 inches (2.5 to 7.5 cm) long; cut plants back in the fall and mulch. Use fresh, dried, frozen, or to flavor vinegar.

Thyme

Thymus spp.

Belonging to the mint family and rich in volatile oils, thyme has made a mark on many cultures through the ages. Its aromatic quality is used in almost any savory dish, and something in its essence seems to bring the other flavors in a dish together. The fruit- and spice-flavored thymes can even be used in desserts.

With well over three hundred species and untold hybrids existing, shopping for thymes can be intimidating. All thymes are edible; but some are better for cooking than others, and they vary with climate and soil. The basic cooking thyme is *T. vulgaris*. Many nurseries offer their own personal selection. Two generally offered are 'Narrowleaf French', with grey-green leaves, and 'Narrowleaf English', with dark green leaves. With a rich scent of lemons, lemon thyme (*T. X citriodorus*) is popular; several other thymes are also lemon-scented, but this is the best. White- or yellow-variegated forms of all these are available. Caraway (*T. herba-barona*), nutmeg (*T. herba-barona 'Nutmeg'*), orange balsam (*T. vulgaris 'Orange Balsam'*), and coconut (*T. praecox 'Coconut'*) thymes speak for themselves as to scent.

Sweet woodruff has a strong aroma and may be used in white wine.

How to grow. Perennials hardy to -20° F (-28.9° C); full sun; ground-hugging to 12 inches (30.5 cm); rounded leaves 1/4 to 1/2 inch (60 to 100 mm) across; white, pink, or lilac flowers in midsummer; mulch in winter in colder climates; grow pots indoors in bright light during the winter. Use as needed fresh during the summer; preserve by drying or freezing.

Thyme is an herb for uniting diverse flavors and foods.

Violet

Viola odorata

Said to have sprung from where Orpheus slept, violets give color to salads of greens or fruits as well as punches, wines, fruit drinks, vinegars, and jellies. Fresh or candied, they decorate cookies, cakes, and pastries. Steeped in spirits, they create *parfait amour*. Make a syrup with them to flavor puddings, ice creams, sorbets, and mousses. Use the fresh leaves in green salads and both leaves and flowers as garnish. Among the varieties available, the double Parma violets are particularly fragrant. Be sure to grow some of the related pansies and Johnny-jump-ups for use as edible flowers.

How to grow. Perennial hardy to -20° F (-28.9° C); light shade; clumps to 6 inches (15 cm) tall; dark green, heart-shaped leaves; purple, lavender, blue, pink, rose, and white flowers. Use flowers fresh, candied, or in syrup, vinegar, or liqueur.

Watercress

Nasturtium officinale

The crisp, dark green leaves with the slightly bitter and peppery bite so excellent for salads, sandwiches, and soups can be homegrown even without a clear-running stream. But not without a price, of course. Pots must be set in pans of water that is changed daily.

Watercress is native to Europe but naturalized over much of the world. It is best in the spring and early summer before flowering gets too far underway, but those in cooler climates can harvest for much of the growing season.

How to grow. Perennial hardy to -30° F (-34.5° C), but also grown as an annual; full sun; divided, rounded leaves to 12 inches (30.5 cm) tall; small white flowers. Use leaves fresh.

Appetizers

Mussels Marinated with Anise Flavors
Cherry Tomatoes Stuffed with Green Bean and Savory Puree
Smoked Trout and Horseradish Cream

Americans love to graze and snack, whether mingling with dozens of people at a party or sitting alone in front of the television. Although appetizers are intended literally "to stimulate the appetite before a meal," they play a much broader role. Dishes like the mussels or asparagus spears are simple, elegant first courses, coming close to the definition, flavorful yet not rich or filling. Chilled ones like the chicken spread, trout cream, and stuffed cherry tomatoes are finger foods easily made ahead. Served hot, the croustades, turnovers, and grilled chicken nuggets are equally suited to casual eating and celebrations. The vegetable pâté might be a first course or the main course of a light meal, perhaps with a clear soup.

None of these would have as much character without their herbal seasoning, but it is the ubiquitous dips and cheeses that stand the most to gain. With the emphasis on herbs they can be made with almost no fat and still have great flavor.

Use purees of vegetables, such as tomatoes, green beans, eggplant, or different-colored peppers, for dips and sauces. Try different kinds of cheese and herb combinations. Low-fat ricotta or homemade yogurt cheese is adaptable to many uses, as are the wonderful American goat cheeses. One of the award-winning cheeses made by Capriole in Greenville, Indiana, melds cheddar with pesto, dried tomatoes, and pine nuts.

Herb toast is another readily made appetizer that is simple to prepare yet makes any occasion seem a bit more special. Using day-old loaves of Italian bread, cut 1-inch-thick slices on a diagonal. Split a fresh garlic clove in half and rub the bread with the cut surface. Brush the bread with extra virgin olive oil or an herb-flavored oil. Sprinkle with freshly grated Parmesan or Romano cheese mixed with minced fresh herbs. Toast under a broiler until golden.

Note: To substitute dried herbs for fresh, lessen quantities by one-half to two-thirds.

SAVORY HERB CHEESE

Makes about 1 cup

Fresh cheeses, whether from goat or cow, rich in cream or a low-fat version, form a perfect partnership with countless herb mixtures. For a simple appetizer, serve them with bread, crackers, or a platter of raw vegetables. With time and inclination, they fill omelets, crepes, and ravioli. However they're used, they satisfy with their fresh, intense flavor, dictated only by imagination and what the garden yields.

For openers, consider combinations of parsley, chives, and thyme; basil, dill, and chives; jalapeños and cilantro; sage and shallots; chervil and tarragon; lemon thyme and mint; parsley and summer savory; arugula and burnet; fennel and sweet cicely; burnet, horseradish, chives, and parsley; or lemon basil and marjoram.

**Herbs, flowers, and vegetables
are attractive companions in a backyard garden.**

*8 ounces regular or light cream cheese,
regular or light ricotta cheese, fresh goat cheese, or
homemade yogurt cheese(see note) at room temperature*

1 garlic clove, minced

¼ cup minced fresh herb leaves

3 tablespoons minced Niçoise or Kalamata olives (optional)

¼ cup finely chopped toasted nuts (see page 69; optional)

By hand or in a food processor, blend all the ingredients. Chill, allowing the flavors to blend for at least a day before serving.

N o t e : To make yogurt cheese, use a commercially available yogurt strainer or line a bowl with several layers of cheesecloth or a thin cotton kitchen towel and pour in 1 quart nonfat or low-fat yogurt, using a brand containing no gelatin. Gather the corners and tie firmly. Suspend the bag over the bowl or sink and let drip overnight. If desired, keep the whey to use in baking. Use the cheese or refrigerate. Makes about 2 cups, or about 1 pound. This will keep for about a week.

CREAM CHEESE
PASTRY TURNOVERS
WITH RED CABBAGE AND
POPPY SEEDS

Makes 36 turnovers

Many of the settlers of the Great American Plains were of Slavic origin, and much of the home cooking of this region reflects that heritage. These sturdy pastries represent three elements of this melting-pot culinary legacy—piroshki, poppy seeds, and cooked red cabbage. The nutty flavor of the poppy seeds complements the engaging tang of the cream cheese pastry and the red cabbage, which is milder tasting than the green type.

For the cream cheese pastry

8 ounces light cream cheese, at room temperature

*½ cup (1 stick) unsalted butter or margarine,
at room temperature*

*1½ cups unbleached or whole wheat
all-purpose flour*

For the filling

2 tablespoons vegetable oil, preferably canola

1 small red onion, finely chopped

*1 small (about ½ pound) red cabbage,
quartered, cored, and finely shredded*

1 medium-size carrot, grated

3 radishes, grated

*1 small apple, such as Golden Delicious or Granny Smith,
cored and grated*

1 garlic clove, minced

½ cup chopped walnuts

2 tablespoons balsamic vinegar

1 teaspoon grated horseradish

1 tablespoon poppy seeds

½ teaspoon salt

Freshly ground black pepper to taste

For the pastry, mix the cream cheese and butter together in a medium-size bowl or food processor. Add the flour and blend thoroughly. Cover the dough with plastic wrap and refrigerate for 30 minutes.

Preheat the oven to 350°F.

For the filling, heat the oil over medium-high heat in a large nonstick skillet. Add the onion and cook, stirring,

Neat rows of antique willowware, pressed glass, and pewter impart a sense of order and well-being.

for 1 minute. Add the cabbage and carrot. Cook, stirring occasionally, for 2 minutes. Add the remaining ingredients, lower the heat to medium, and cook, continuing to stir, for 5 minutes. Remove from the heat.

Roll the dough out to 1/8-inch thickness on a lightly floured surface. Cut into rounds with a 3-inch biscuit cutter. Place a tablespoon of the filling on half of each circle, then fold the other half of the circle over the filling. Press the edges together with a fork. Prick the top with the fork to allow steam to escape. Bake on an ungreased baking sheet until lightly browned, 15 to 20 minutes. Serve warm or at room temperature.

CROUSTADES
WITH
MUSHROOM FILLING

Makes 24 croustades

These easily made little tarts pair the woodsy, full-bodied flavor of shiitake and oyster mushrooms with the mild, slightly sweet, oregano-like quality of marjoram. Parsley and chives round out the herbal trio.

24 slices soft whole wheat bread, crusts removed

1 tablespoon unsalted butter or margarine

2 tablespoons virgin or extra virgin olive oil

½ cup finely chopped shallots

1 garlic clove, minced

½ pound fresh shiitake mushrooms, thinly sliced

½ pound fresh oyster mushrooms, thinly sliced

1 tablespoon minced fresh marjoram leaves

1 tablespoon minced fresh parsley leaves

1 teaspoon minced fresh chives

1 cup light ricotta cheese or homemade yogurt cheese (see page 23)

½ teaspoon salt

Freshly ground black pepper to taste

¼ cup freshly grated Parmesan cheese

Preheat the oven to 350°F. With a rolling pin, roll each slice of bread flat. With a pastry brush, lightly brush both sides of each slice with olive oil. Fit the slices of bread into the cups of a standard-size-cup muffin pan. Toast in the oven until golden, about 10 to 12 minutes. Gently remove from the pan and cool the croustades on a wire rack. They can be made up to a week in advance and stored in an airtight container. Reheat, if desired, in a preheated 300°F oven for 5 minutes.

To make the filling, heat the butter and olive oil over medium heat in a large nonstick skillet. Cook the shallots and garlic, stirring, until soft and translucent, about 3 minutes. Add the mushrooms and herbs and cook, over medium-low heat, stirring occasionally, until most of the liquid has evaporated, about 20 to 30 minutes. Stir in the ricotta, then season with salt and pepper. Spoon the mixture into the croustades, sprinkle the Parmesan on top, and serve immediately.

LEMON BASIL, CHICKEN, AND NUT SPREAD

Makes 1 ½ cups

Renee Shepherd of Shepherd's Garden Seeds, Felton, California, creates foods for parties where she's showing off new vegetable, herb, and flower varieties from her mail-order catalog. Inspired by her, this spread can be made into elegant little tea sandwiches, served on a luncheon plate with fresh fruit, or offered at a cocktail party as a spread for crackers or as a filling for Belgian endive leaves. Other flavors of basil can be used, too, especially cinnamon and anise, as well as other nuts, such as pine nuts, almonds, or pistachios.

1 cup water

½ cup dry white wine

¼ cup balsamic vinegar

1 garlic clove, peeled and halved

One 4-inch sprig fresh parsley

1 bay leaf

½ pound skinless, boneless chicken breasts, trimmed of fat

4 ounces light cream cheese or homemade yogurt cheese (see page 23), at room temperature

1 tablespoon honey

1 tablespoon minced fresh lemon basil leaves

½ teaspoon grated lemon zest

⅓ cup finely chopped toasted pecans (see page 69)

Salt and freshly ground black pepper to taste

In a saucepan, combine the water, wine, vinegar, garlic, parsley, and bay leaf and bring to a boil. Reduce the heat to low and simmer for 5 minutes. Add the chicken breasts, cover, and poach gently just until the chicken is no longer pink inside, 6 to 8 minutes. Remove the chicken from the poaching liquid, drain, and chop finely.

Blend the cream cheese and honey until smooth. Stir in the chicken and remaining ingredients. Serve immediately or chill for up to several days. Bring to room temperature before spreading on bread.

Note: For a vegetarian alternative, substitute 1/2 pound drained, finely crumbled, firm or extra-firm tofu for the chicken.

CHERRY TOMATOES STUFFED WITH GREEN BEAN AND SAVORY PUREE

Makes 20 to 24 stuffed tomatoes

Savory has a flavor reminiscent of thyme and mint. An annual, summer savory has a slightly milder flavor than the perennial winter savory so more can be used.

Consider yellow cherry tomato varieties, such as 'Chello' or 'Gold Nugget', the full-flavored red 'Camp Joy', and the prolific red 'Sweet Million'.

20 to 24 cherry tomatoes

½ pound green beans, cut into 2-inch lengths

1 teaspoon minced fresh savory leaves

3 small new red potatoes, quartered

Salt and freshly ground black pepper to taste

Slice off a third of each tomato at the stem end. Use a small melon ball cutter to scoop out the pulp and seeds. Sprinkle them lightly with salt and invert on a towel.

Combine the beans, savory, and potatoes in a saucepan with 1 inch of water. Bring to a boil, cover, and reduce the heat to medium-low. Cook until the potatoes are tender, about 10 minutes. Drain. Puree in a food processor or blender and season with salt and pepper.

Using a pastry bag fitted with a star tip, pipe the puree into the tomatoes. Cover and chill for 1 hour before serving.

TRICOLOR
VEGETABLE PÂTÉ

Makes one 9- by 5-inch loaf

This pâté invites experimentation with different vegetables for each of the layers as well as different herbs. One of the most beautiful of foods, this not only makes an elegant appetizer but could also be the main course of a luncheon or picnic.

For the orange layer

1 pound carrots, sweet potatoes, or winter squash, peeled and thinly sliced

2 large eggs

¼ cup skim milk

2 tablespoons fresh or dried calendula petals

½ teaspoon ground coriander seeds

¼ teaspoon ground cardamom seeds

¼ teaspoon ground ginger

¼ teaspoon salt

Freshly ground black pepper to taste

⅓ cup plain dried bread crumbs or ¼ cup cooked brown rice

For the white layer

4 leeks with 2 inches of green top, roots removed, or 2 cups diced cauliflower and ¼ cup chopped yellow onion

2 tablespoons virgin or extra virgin olive oil

1 garlic clove, minced

2 large eggs

¼ cup skim milk

½ teaspoon crushed caraway seeds

¼ teaspoon salt

Freshly ground black pepper to taste

⅓ cup plain dried bread crumbs or ¼ cup cooked brown rice

For the green layer

1 pound fresh greens, such as spinach, chard, or kale, cleaned and stems removed, or 2½ cups chopped green vegetables, such as green beans, broccoli, asparagus, or peas

2 large eggs

¼ cup skim milk

2 tablespoons minced fresh herb leaves: basil, dill, summer savory, burnet, chervil, chives, garlic chives, or marjoram

⅓ cup plain dried bread crumbs or ¼ cup cooked brown rice

Butter a 9- by 5-inch loaf pan and line with buttered wax paper.

Through the morning mist flowers, vegetables, and herbs glisten.

To make the orange layer, steam the vegetables over medium-low heat until very tender, about 15 minutes, then drain well. Puree in a blender or food processor with the remaining ingredients until smooth. Spoon into the loaf pan, leveling the top.

To make the white layer, cut the leeks in half and rinse out all the dirt. Pat dry and slice thinly. Heat the oil in a large nonstick skillet over medium heat, then cook the leeks and garlic, stirring, until soft, about 15 minutes. Beat the eggs in a bowl and stir in the leeks and remaining ingredients, mixing well. If you're using cauliflower and onion, steam over medium-low heat until tender, then drain well; puree in a blender or food processor with the remaining ingredients until smooth. Gently add to the loaf pan, leveling the top.

To make the green layer, if you're using greens, steam over medium-low heat and squeeze dry or steam the vegetables over medium-low heat until tender, then drain well. Combine with the remaining ingredients in a blender or food processor and puree until smooth. Gently add to the loaf pan, leveling the top. The filling should be about 1/2 inch below the top of the pan.

Preheat the oven to 350°F. Cover the pan with a sheet of buttered wax paper, then a sheet of aluminum foil. Set the pan in a larger pan containing enough hot water to reach halfway up the sides of the loaf pan. Bake for 1 1/4 hours. Insert a knife in the center; if it does not come out clean, bake for another 15 minutes. Cool on a wire rack for 1 hour. Run a knife around the edges of the pan, put a serving plate over it, and invert. Remove the pan and wax paper. Let cool for another 30 minutes, then cover and chill for up to several days. Serve on chilled greens with an herb mayonnaise or a sauce made from pureed red peppers and onions.

ASPARAGUS WITH LEMON THYME AND SMOKED TURKEY

Makes about 20 pieces

My first choice for eating asparagus is simply steaming it lightly and eating it with nothing more than a squeeze of fresh lemon. For a meal or party when I want to do a little more, I stay with lemon flavors but enriched with thinly sliced smoked turkey and the delicate flavor of lemon thyme, an herb that should be in every garden. If you have any yard space at all, consider growing your own asparagus since it is a long-lived perennial with almost no pests.

1 pound asparagus

About 20 very thin slices smoked turkey

3 tablespoons minced fresh lemon thyme leaves

Freshly ground black pepper to taste

2 tablespoons fresh lemon juice

1 tablespoon virgin or extra virgin olive oil

Preheat the oven to 350°F.

Trim the tough ends off the asparagus stalks. Place the stalks in the top half of a steamer with an inch of water in the bottom. Cover and bring the water to a boil. Cook until crisp-tender, 5 to 6 minutes.

Sprinkle a slice of the smoked turkey with a little of the lemon thyme and wrap it around an asparagus spear. Place in a baking pan. Repeat with the remaining asparagus. Season with pepper and drizzle with lemon juice and olive oil. Bake, uncovered, for 8 minutes. Serve hot or at room temperature. If available, garnish with fresh lemon thyme flowers, which are a lovely pale lilac.

PEPPER DIP WITH PARSLEY AND LOVAGE

Makes 1 cup

For a change from dips based on dairy products, this thick, intensely colored one has vegetables as the central ingredient. Sweet red peppers that demand premium prices at the grocery can be enjoyed fresh from the garden for several months during the summer if you allow green peppers to ripen. The French hybrid variety 'Vidi' is a Lamuyo form such as those marketed as 'La Rouge Royale'. 'Italia' is an early-ripening form of the long sweet Italian bull's horn pepper.

Besides serving this dip with a platter of raw vegetables, it also makes a fine sauce for steamed vegetables or grilled chicken or fish.

1 tablespoon virgin or extra virgin olive oil

½ cup finely diced onion

2 cups (about 3 medium-size) cored, seeded, and chopped red bell peppers

1 small fresh red jalapeño or other hot pepper, cored, seeded, and minced

1 tablespoon minced fresh parsley leaves

1 teaspoon minced fresh lovage leaves

½ teaspoon salt

½ cup vegetable stock (see page 36) or dry white wine

In a large skillet, heat the oil over medium heat. Add the onion and cook, stirring, for 2 minutes. Add the remaining ingredients. Bring to a boil, reduce the heat to low, and simmer, uncovered, until the liquid has evaporated and the peppers are very soft, about 20 minutes.

Using a food processor or blender, process the mixture until smooth. Chill before serving.

MUSSELS MARINATED WITH ANISE FLAVORS

Makes 4 to 6 servings

Mussels have long been a favorite food of mine because they deliver great flavor at little expense. Low in calories, mussels are a source of Omega-3 fatty acids, which have been shown to help reduce blood cholesterol.

Mussels have undergone a change in the last several decades as research has determined how to grow them under somewhat controlled conditions. Aquacultured mussels reach market size in 18 months as opposed to 8 years for wild mussels, and they are meatier, more uniform in size, and do not have the tiny nuisance pearls that wild mussels contain.

Each of the herbs used in this dish has the flavor of anise but with softer tones. If you don't have all three, use just one or two, increasing their amounts.

For the mussels

2 pounds mussels in the shell

1 cup dry white wine

¼ cup anise liqueur

2 tablespoons fresh lemon juice

2 shallots or 1 small yellow onion, chopped

2 garlic cloves, crushed

One 4-inch fresh chervil sprig

One 4-inch fresh fennel sprig

One 4-inch fresh tarragon sprig

For the salsa with anise flavors

*2 cups ripe tomatoes, peeled and seeded (see note),
then finely chopped (about 1 pound)*

3 tablespoons virgin or extra virgin olive oil

1 teaspoon minced fresh chervil leaves

1 teaspoon minced fresh fennel leaves

1 teaspoon minced fresh tarragon leaves

*1 tablespoon minced fresh garlic chives
or 1 small garlic clove, minced*

2 tablespoons tarragon-white wine vinegar

1 teaspoon fresh lemon juice

Salt and freshly ground black pepper to taste

Sort through the mussels and discard any that remain open after their shells are tapped. Scrub the mussels under cold running water, pulling off the beards.

Combine the remaining ingredients for the mussels in a large pot and bring to a boil. Add the mussels, cover, and steam until the mussels open, 6 to 8 minutes, discarding any that have not opened. Drain the mussels and remove them from their shells, keeping and rinsing the shells.

In a bowl, combine the salsa ingredients and gently stir in the mussels. Cover and chill for 1 to 6 hours. To serve, spoon a mussel with some of the salsa onto each half shell. Garnish the plates with sprigs of fresh herbs.

Note: To peel and seed tomatoes, dip them into boiling water for 20 to 30 seconds, remove, and pull off the skins with the aid of a paring knife. Cut the tomatoes in half horizontally, hold each half over a bowl, cut side down, and squeeze to remove the seeds.

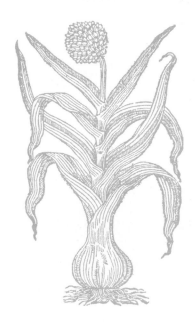

SMOKED TROUT
AND HORSERADISH
CREAM

Makes 1 ½ cups filling

Smoked trout and horseradish are a pairing of long standing, with the other herbs adding grace notes in the background. Using a star-shaped pastry tip, you can pipe this mixture onto Belgian endive leaves, cucumber or zucchini slices, yellow pear tomato halves, hard-cooked egg halves, snap pea pods, or tiny puff pastry shells. These hors d'oeurves can be made up to 8 hours ahead of serving and stored, covered, in the refrigerator.

In spring and early summer I prefer to fill snap pea pods. 'Sugar Daddy' is a stringless variety with good flavor and production on plants whose 24- to 30-inch height is more manageable than the 6-foot vines of the original 'Sugar Snap' pea developed in Idaho.

½ pound smoked trout, skin removed

*8 ounces light cream cheese
or homemade yogurt cheese (see page 23)*

¼ cup nonfat or low-fat plain yogurt

¼ cup reduced-calorie or low-fat mayonnaise

1 tablespoon grated horseradish

2 tablespoons minced fresh dill leaves

1 teaspoon minced fresh tarragon leaves

2 teaspoons fresh lemon juice

Freshly ground black pepper to taste

Fresh dill sprigs

In a food processor, combine all the ingredients except the dill sprigs and process until smooth. Use the dill sprigs to garnish the finished hors d'oeuvres.

A split-rail fence barely contains the daylilies, iris, and herbs at an herb farm.

GRILLED CHICKEN NUGGETS WITH ASIAN MARINADE

Makes about 40 pieces

This version of an Indonesian satay uses almond butter rather than the traditional peanut butter and relies on the unique flavor of cilantro to balance the hot spices. Supposedly the world's most widely used herb, cilantro (fresh coriander) is also known as *Chinese parsley*. Plants mature quickly, so replant every 2 to 4 weeks and allow some to go to seed to save you the trouble.

Shoyu is a Japanese soy sauce that is lower in salt; it is available at health food stores, as is the almond butter.

3 tablespoons almond butter

1 garlic clove, minced

1 quarter-size piece fresh ginger, peeled and minced

2 tablespoons shoyu

¼ cup dry sherry

½ teaspoon hot red pepper sauce or ground cayenne pepper

1 teaspoon minced fresh coriander (cilantro) leaves

1 tablespoon minced fresh parsley leaves

1 pound boneless, skinless chicken breast, cut into 1-inch pieces

Lettuce

Thoroughly combine all the ingredients except the chicken and lettuce in a bowl. Add the chicken pieces and stir gently to coat well. Cover and chill for 6 hours. Soak wooden skewers in water for 30 minutes. Thread the chicken pieces on to the skewers and grill or broil, turning as necessary, just until cooked, 10 minutes. Remove from the skewers and serve on a platter lined with lettuce leaves or on individual plates with a bed of lettuce chiffonnade.

Soups

Green Tomato Soup with Garlic, Ginger, Cumin, and Coriander

One time after about four days of taking my visiting parents to favorite restaurants and making recommendations, my mother asked if we could have something besides soup. Such are my predilections, whether hot or cold, creamy or clear, broth or stew. With a bowl of soup, great bread, and a crisp salad one might ask little more of life, at least culinarily.

Stock serves as the framework for the soup. Without quality stock, soup may be good but will not be great. Granted life is hectic and full, but homemade vegetable stock is low in cost, low in fat, and healthy. It is also quickly prepared or, if necessary, can be made ahead and frozen. When totally pressed for time, use commercially canned vegetable or chicken stock with no additives. Stock is very personal and as variable from day to day as the ingredients and soup command. For inspiration on the many ways to make vegetable stock I turn to The Greens Cook Book.

First, choose the ingredients to reflect the soup in which the stock is being used. A general guideline for making vegetable stock is to use about 8 to 12 cups of vegetables cut into pieces no bigger than 1 inch. Put these with 2 quarts of cold water in a large nonreactive pot with no more than six different herbs. Bring to a boil over high heat, then lower the heat and simmer for 30 to 45 minutes. Strain and use as is or concentrate the flavor by simmering to the desired strength.

The basic ingredients to consider including in a vegetable stock are onions or leeks, carrots, celery, potatoes, winter and summer squash, chard, kale, tomatoes, mushrooms, eggplant, lettuce, green beans, and celeriac. When appropriate, use fennel bulbs, asparagus, or peas. Cabbage family members often give a strong, unpleasant flavor, so use them cautiously.

For herbs, there's basil, bay, borage, garlic, garlic chives, hyssop, lovage, marjoram, oregano, parsley, sage, savory, and thyme in various combinations, but consider others, too. For spicy soups, try coriander, cumin, cardamom, or fennel seeds, whole cloves, or a cinnamon stick.

Note: To substitute dried herbs for fresh, lessen quantities by one-half to two-thirds.

HOT AND SOUR GARLIC CHIVE SOUP WITH TOFU

Makes 2 to 4 servings

Since garlic, or Chinese, chives are one of the first plants up in the spring and one of the last to die back in the fall, and they have a subtle flavor combining, obviously, that of garlic and chives, I find them indispensable in just about anything but dessert. Plus, the flowers are lovely to look at both in the garden and in bouquets as well as great to eat. In other words, an altogether superb herb.

Most of the the Asian ingredients are available in supermarkets as well as in Asian markets and health food stores.

Luscious tomatoes and crisp lettuces, grown in the vegetable garden at an inn, supply the chef with ingredients for succulent salads and flavorful soup stocks.

2 medium-size carrots, sliced

¼ cup minced fresh garlic chives or chives and 1 garlic clove

3 fresh lovage or celery leaves

3 romaine lettuce or Swiss chard leaves, torn into pieces

4 dried cloud ear or shiitake mushrooms

One 6-inch piece dried arame, dulse, or kombu seaweed

1 small fresh or dried hot red pepper

2 tablespoons rice wine vinegar

1 quart water

1 cup dry white wine

1 teaspoon dark (Chinese) sesame oil

½ pound firm tofu, cut into ½-inch pieces

2 tablespoons rice or barley miso

Garlic chive leaves or flowers

In a large heavy pot, combine all the ingredients except the tofu, miso, and chive leaves. Bring to a boil, then cover, lower the heat to medium-low, and simmer for 30 minutes. Remove the mushrooms and slice thinly, discarding the tough portions. Strain the broth and return it to the pan. Add the tofu and mushrooms and simmer for 5 minutes. Dissolve the miso in a small amount of the broth, stir it into the soup, then immediately remove the pot from the heat. Garnish with minced garlic chive leaves and serve at once.

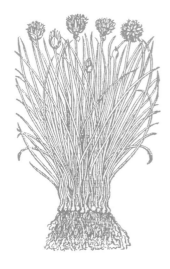

SPICY LEEK SOUP WITH SAGE AND PARSLEY

Makes 4 to 6 servings

Both leeks and sweet potatoes are winter vegetables and good sources of calcium, phosphorus, and vitamin A; the latter is also rich in B and C vitamins.

Sage is an ingredient often pigeonholed into certain uses and seldom otherwise considered. Having a natural affinity for cheese and onions means it adapts well to this combination of ingredients. Use this soup either as the main feature of a light lunch or supper with a salad or as the first course with a pork or chicken entree.

To make sure you get all the soil out of the leeks, slice them in half lengthwise, then take the leaves out one by one and wash thoroughly.

1 tablespoon unsalted butter or margarine

2 tablespoons virgin or extra virgin olive oil

3 large leeks, both white and tender green parts,
well washed, and thinly sliced

¼ cup minced shallots

1 pound sweet potatoes, peeled and diced

3 cups vegetable stock (see page 36),
canned vegetable broth, or bouillon cubes

1 tablespoon minced fresh sage leaves

2 tablepoons minced fresh parsley leaves

1 small fresh or dried hot red pepper

1 cup skim milk

½ cup freshly grated Monterey Jack cheese

Salt and freshly ground black pepper to taste

Minced fresh parsley, fresh nasturtium flowers,
or fresh or dried calendula petals

In a large saucepan, heat the butter and oil over medium heat, then add the leeks and shallots and cook, stirring, until soft and translucent, about 10 minutes. Add the sweet potatoes, stock, sage, parsley, and hot pepper. Bring to a boil, reduce the heat to low, cover, and simmer until the potatoes are tender, about 20 to 30 minutes. Remove the hot pepper. In a food processor or blender, puree the soup in batches. Return to the saucepan and stir in the milk. Heat just to a simmer, then stir in the cheese until melted. Remove from the heat and add salt and pepper. Serve garnished with minced parsley, nasturtium flowers, or calendula petals.

BAKED GARLIC SOUP WITH HERB TOAST

Makes 4 servings

Long, slow baking of garlic transforms its bite into a sweet paste bearing little resemblance to fresh garlic. Besides its use in this soup, the paste can be added to mashed potatoes, served with meats or vegetables, or simply spread on slices of toasted Italian bread for a classic appetizer.

1 whole garlic head

1 tablespoon virgin or extra virgin olive oil;
plus extra for the toasts

1 tablespoon balsamic vinegar or brandy

One 3-inch fresh rosemary sprig

3 cups vegetable stock (see page 36),
canned vegetable broth, or bouillon cubes

½ cup dry white wine or sherry

Salt and freshly ground black pepper to taste

For the herb toast

½ loaf whole wheat Italian bread,
cut diagonally into ½-inch-thick slices

1 garlic clove, peeled and
cut in half lengthwise

Extra virgin olive oil

½ cup freshly grated Parmesan cheese

1 tablespoon fresh garlic chives, minced

Preheat the oven to 300°F. Slice the top from the head of garlic and remove most of the papery outer skin from the head, but do not peel or separate into cloves. Place in a small ovenproof dish. Pour the olive oil over the top and add the vinegar and rosemary. Cover with aluminum foil and bake until very tender, about 1 hour. Remove from the oven and let cool.

Preheat the oven to 350°F. Squeeze the softened garlic from the skins into a saucepan, and add the stock and wine. Heat to a simmer over medium-low heat and cook for 15 minutes. While cooking, make the herb toast. Bake the bread slices on a baking sheet until crisp but not golden, 6 to 8 minutes. Rub the bread with the cut sides of the garlic clove, then brush generously with oil. Sprinkle on a thin layer of the Parmesan cheese and chives. Bake until the cheese is melted, another 5 minutes. Serve immediately with the hot soup.

The dim, dusty light of an old barn reveals a handmade wooden rake,
left, as well as grain and hay for the animals in the winter.

Soups and other foods with a distinctive blend of flavors benefit from long, slow cooking
and must be stirred continually.

SHAKER
FRESH HERB SOUP

Makes 4 servings

Never numbering more than six thousand, the United Society for Believers in Christ's Second Appearing, better known as Shakers, have had a pronounced impact on American life. They started the first commercial herb industry in the United States and sold both dried herbs, mainly for medicinal use, and herb seeds. Among the innovations we owe the Shakers is the packing of seeds for sale in small envelopes.

Shakers were copious record keepers and one such record, *Sister Amelia's Shaker Receipts*, yields this recipe for a spring soup, which carries on the European heritage of using the first fresh herbs of the year as part of the Easter ritual and also as a health-restoring tonic.

1 tablespoon unsalted butter or margarine

2 tablespoons minced fresh chives

2 tablespoons minced fresh chervil leaves

2 tablespoons minced fresh sorrel leaves

½ teaspoon minced fresh tarragon leaves

1 cup finely chopped celery ribs

*1 quart vegetable stock (see page 36),
canned vegetable broth, or bouillon cubes*

Salt and freshly ground black pepper to taste

Pinch of sugar

4 slices whole wheat toast

Dash of freshly grated nutmeg

Grated cheddar cheese

Melt the butter over medium heat in a large heavy pot. Add the herbs and celery and cook, stirring, until wilted and soft, about 3 minutes. Add the stock, salt, pepper, and sugar. Bring to a boil, reduce the heat to low, cover, and simmer for 20 minutes. Place a slice of toast in each soup bowl and pour the soup over. Dust with nutmeg and sprinkle with grated cheese.

CARROT AND
WILD RICE SOUP
WITH THYME
AND CALENDULA

Makes 6 servings

Grown fresh at home or bought dried at a health food store, calendula petals, once omnipresent in medieval cooking, are worth the effort for their bright color and peppery flavor. Nasturtium flowers would be an admirable alternative.

2 tablespoons vegetable oil, preferably canola

1 large leek, white part only, well washed and thinly sliced

2 garlic cloves, minced

2 medium-size celery ribs, finely chopped

½ pound mushrooms, thinly sliced

1 pound carrots, diced

*1 quart vegetable stock (see page 36),
canned vegetable broth, or bouillon cubes*

½ cup fresh orange juice

½ cup dry sherry

1 tablespoon minced fresh thyme leaves

¼ cup minced fresh or dried calendula petals

1 bay leaf

1 cup cooked wild rice

Salt and freshly ground black pepper to taste

Heat the oil over medium heat in a large heavy pot, then add the leeks and garlic and cook, stirring, until the leeks are translucent, about 5 minutes. Stir in the celery, mushrooms, and carrots and cook for 10 minutes, stirring often. Add the stock, orange juice, sherry, thyme, calendula petals, and bay leaf. Bring to a boil, reduce the heat to low, cover, and simmer until the carrots are tender, 20 to 25 minutes. Remove the bay leaf, stir in the wild rice, and let simmer for another 5 minutes. Season with salt and pepper and serve.

SOUTHWESTERN SOUP

Makes 4 to 6 servings

A New World soup that relies on ingredients indigenous to this continent, it traditionally varies from cook to cook and from day to day, depending on what's at hand. At any given time one might use carrots, summer squash, or green beans instead of the corn and red bell pepper. Different kinds of hot peppers could be used; shredded cooked chicken, rice, or grated cheese might be added. Extra stock makes for a lighter soup. Or eliminate the tortillas and serve with corn bread.

Hand-thrown pots wait for the kiln, where they will be fired and then used for generations.

2 tablespoons vegetable oil, preferably canola

⅔ cup chopped yellow onion

1 garlic clove, minced

1 teaspoon ground cumin

1 tablespoon minced fresh oregano leaves

1 small jalapeño pepper, cored, seeded, and minced

1 medium-size red bell pepper, cored, seeded, and minced

1 quart vegetable stock (see page 36), canned vegetable broth, or bouillon cubes

1 cup cooked corn, fresh or frozen

¼ cup fresh lime juice

2 cups drained cooked white beans or one 16-ounce can, drained and rinsed (see page 47)

1 cup peeled and seeded (see page 31), then chopped, tomatoes

1 medium-size avocado, peeled, pitted, chopped, and tossed with a little lime juice to prevent discoloration

3 tablespoons minced fresh coriander (cilantro) leaves

Salt and freshly ground black pepper to taste

Four 6-inch corn tortillas, cut into ½-inch strips

Heat 1 tablespoon of the oil over medium heat in a large heavy pot. Add the onion, garlic, cumin, oregano, jalapeño, and bell pepper and cook, stirring, until the onion is transparent, 6 to 8 minutes. Add the stock and bring to a boil. Reduce the heat to low, cover, and simmer for 20 minutes. Add the corn, lime juice, and beans and bring back to a simmer. Add the tomatoes, avocado, and cilantro and remove from the heat. Season with salt and pepper.

While the soup is simmering, heat the remaining oil in a nonstick skillet over medium-high heat, then fry the tortilla strips until crisp, about 3 to 5 minutes. Drain on towels. Put several strips in each bowl, then pour in the soup.

SORREL AND ASPARAGUS SOUP

Makes 4 servings

Spring is a ritualistic time for me, when my pantheistic nature holds full sway. Some of my earliest memories are of springtime forays into woods, fields, and garden, searching out the first pale lavender hepatica blooms, elusive morels, mouth-puckering sorrel leaves, or bold spears of asparagus.

1 tablespoon virgin or extra virgin olive oil

⅓ cup minced shallots

1 cup peeled and diced new potato

*2 cups vegetable stock (see page 36)
or canned vegetable broth*

½ pound asparagus, cut into 1-inch pieces

2 cups chopped fresh sorrel leaves

1 tablespoon minced fresh lovage or celery leaves

1 cup skim milk

2 tablespoons minced fresh chervil leaves

Salt and freshly ground black pepper to taste

Croutons, nonfat or low-fat plain yogurt, or chive blossoms

Heat the oil over medium heat in a large heavy nonreactive pot, then add the shallots and cook, stirring, until transparent, about 3 minutes. Add the potatoes and stock. Bring to a boil, reduce the heat to low, and simmer for 15 minutes. Add the asparagus and cook until the potatoes and asparagus are tender, about 10 minutes. Stir in the sorrel and lovage and cook for another 3 minutes. In a food processor or blender, puree the soup in batches until smooth. Return it to the pot and stir in the milk, chervil, salt, and pepper. Heat just to a boil. Remove from the heat and serve or allow to cool, then chill before serving. Garnish with croutons or a dollop of yogurt and chive blossom petals.

CUCUMBER SOUP WITH BURNET AND ALMONDS

Makes 4 servings

The archetypal revitalizing food for torrid summer days, a cold soup of cucumbers and yogurt is a concept centuries old that spans cultures from India to countries of the Middle East, Balkans, eastern Mediterranean, and northward to Scandinavia.

Ideally, choose a variety of nonbitter cucumber. The easiest one to grow is Park's 'Burpless Bush'. This one does well in containers and starts producing cucumbers less than two months after planting.

Burnet is a graceful perennial herb with feathery leaves having the taste of cucumbers. Using some of this herb fresh emphasizes the flavor of the soup, while mint and dill complement it.

3 cups peeled, seeded, and grated cucumbers (about 2)

1 garlic clove, minced, or 1 tablespoon garlic chives

¼ cup thinly sliced scallions, both white and green parts

2 tablespoons mint or white wine vinegar

1½ cups buttermilk

1½ cups nonfat or low-fat plain yogurt

*½ cup minced fresh herb leaves: burnet, mint, dill,
or a combination*

½ cup toasted slivered almonds (see page 69)

In a large bowl, combine the cucumbers, garlic, scallions, vinegar, buttermilk, yogurt, and 1/4 cup of the fresh herbs. For a smooth soup, the ingredients can be pureed in a blender or food processor. Cover and refrigerate at least 4 hours before serving. Pour into serving bowls and garnish with the remaining herbs and the toasted almonds.

GREEN TOMATO SOUP WITH GARLIC, GINGER, CUMIN, AND CORIANDER

Makes 4 servings

This soup, with its warming, redolent combination of herbs and spices, makes a great first course or light meal for those crisply beautiful autumn days. In fact, you may want to make it throughout the growing season, serving it chilled during summer's hottest days.

3 tablespoons virgin or extra virgin olive oil

1 cup chopped yellow onions

1 teaspoon minced fresh ginger

1 garlic clove, minced

1 teaspoon ground coriander

2 teaspoons ground cumin

1½ pounds green tomatoes, peeled and seeded (see page 31), then chopped

1 medium-size green bell pepper, cored, seeded, and chopped

½ pound boiling potatoes, diced (about 1½ cups)

2 cups vegetable stock (see page 36), canned vegetable broth, or bouillon cubes

1 tablespoon honey

1 small fresh or dried hot red pepper

½ cup unsweetened coconut milk or skim milk

½ teaspoon salt

¼ cup nonfat or low-fat plain yogurt

¼ cup toasted chopped unsalted cashews (see page 69)

4 teaspoons minced fresh coriander (cilantro) leaves

In a large heavy pot, heat the oil over medium heat, then add the onions, ginger, garlic, coriander, and cumin and cook, stirring, until the onions are soft and translucent, about 5 minutes. Add the tomatoes, bell pepper, potatoes, stock, honey, and hot pepper. Bring to a boil, reduce the heat to low, and simmer, covered, for 30 minutes. Remove the hot pepper. Using a blender or food processor, puree the soup in batches. Return it to the pot, stir in the coconut milk and salt, then heat just to a simmer. Serve garnished with dollop of yogurt, cashews, and cilantro.

Herb gardens all around the country welcome visitors to come and learn.

GAZPACHO WITH WATERCRESS AND ARUGULA

Makes 6 to 8 servings

The arugula and watercress add an especially bright taste to this summertime classic. Do I have to say that this is a soup to be made from sun-ripened tomatoes, not the rock-hard, grocery store type? Those who don't like the southwestern flavors of jalapeño and cilantro can leave them out, but what a pity.

¾ cup whole wheat bread crumbs

2 garlic cloves, minced

2 tablespoons red wine vinegar

½ cup cold water

4 cups peeled and seeded (see page 31),
then finely chopped, tomatoes (about 2 pounds)

1 medium-size green bell pepper, cored, seeded,
and finely chopped

1 medium-size red bell pepper, cored, seeded,
and finely chopped

1 small jalapeño pepper, cored, seeded,
and finely chopped

*1 cup peeled, seeded, and finely chopped
cucumber (1 small)*

1 cup tomato juice

*¼ cup finely sliced scallions,
both white and green parts*

⅓ cup finely chopped red onion

2 tablespoons minced fresh parsley leaves

½ cup minced watercress leaves

½ cup minced fresh arugula leaves

¼ cup minced fresh coriander (cilantro) leaves

2 tablespoons minced fresh lovage or celery leaves

2 tablespoons minced fresh chives

¼ cup virgin or extra virgin olive oil

1 teaspoon salt

Croutons

In a large bowl, combine the bread crumbs, garlic, vinegar, and water. The vegetables can be chopped in a food processor (but not a blender), but because they often end up getting pureed instead, consider doing half in the food processor and half by hand. Combine all the remaining ingredients except croutons in the bowl with the bread-crumb mixture. Cover and chill for at least 4 hours before serving. Garnish with croutons.

VEGETARIAN CHILI

Makes 6 servings

One of my most-used cookbooks is *Wings of Life* by Julie Jordan. Over the years I've made numerous variations of her satisfying chili.

If using canned beans, rinse and drain them in a sieve before adding. To cook your own, soak 1 cup of dry beans overnight in water to cover. The next day, drain any remaining water, add fresh water to cover by 2 inches, cover and cook over medium-low heat until tender, about 1 1/2 hours. Drain before adding to chili.

¼ cup vegetable oil, preferably canola

3 medium-size yellow onions, chopped

2 medium-size green bell peppers, cored, seeded, and chopped

1 medium-size celery rib, finely chopped

1 cup diced carrots

2 garlic cloves, minced

2 teaspoons minced fresh oregano leaves

2 teaspoons minced fresh thyme leaves

1 tablespoon minced fresh lovage leaves

2 teaspoons ground red chili pepper or to taste

1 teaspoon ground cumin

One 28-ounce can or 1 quart home-canned tomatoes

½ cup dry red wine

1 bay leaf

1 cup unsalted cashews

¼ cup raisins

*4 cups cooked kidney or pinto beans or
two 16-ounce cans of cooked beans*

1 teaspoon salt

1 tablespoon minced fresh basil leaves

*2 tablespoons vinegar, preferably a homemade mixed-herb
or red wine vinegar*

Freshly grated cheddar, Colby, or Monterey Jack cheese

Corn bread

Heat the oil over medium heat in a large heavy pot, then add the onions, bell peppers, celery, carrots, and garlic and cook, stirring, until the onions are translucent, 8 to 10 minutes. Add the oregano, thyme, lovage, chili pepper, and cumin and cook for another 3 minutes. Stir in the tomatoes, breaking them up with a spoon. Add the wine, the pepper, bay leaf, cashews, raisins, beans, and salt. Bring to a boil, cover, reduce the heat to low, and simmer for 1 hour. If the chili seems too thick, add some water. Stir in the basil and vinegar and heat for another 5 minutes. Serve with grated cheese and warm corn bread.

Main Courses

If I had a magic lamp, one of my wishes would be for people to feel freer to experiment with their herbs in cooking—not abandoning the traditional combinations but being willing to try something different. Take a recipe, see what's in the garden, then substitute away or add herbs where none are called for.

Nowhere is cooking more open to choices than with grilling. Given that there is as much contention over the best ways to grill as over whether the 1927 Yankees or the 1934 Cardinals were the better team, I'll go out on a limb and give some suggestions, drawing in part from my friend A. Cort Sinnes, author of The Grilling Book.

For meats that don't require tenderizing, especially the more delicate fish, all that is needed is a 30-minute immersion in an herb-infused oil. Drain or lightly wipe the meat before putting it on the grill so that none drips into the coals.

For tougher meats, like flank steak, or to give extra flavor to foods like chicken or lamb chops, use a marinade that penetrates the food. This means a mixture that includes lots of minced herbs with equal parts of an oil and an acidic liquid, such as wine, vinegar, fruit juice, yogurt, or buttermilk. Asian marinades rely on shoyu, a type of soy sauce, and herbs, perhaps with dry sherry, and may or may not contain oil. Marinate meats for as little as 2 hours at room temperature to as long as overnight refrigerated, but bring to room temperature before grilling.

Dry marinades are herb and spice mixtures that are rubbed into the meat surface and left on, refrigerated, for 4 to 6 hours. Make into a thick paste with a little olive oil or coat the meat lightly with oil before applying the dry mixture. Combine 10 or so dried herbs and spices and use 6 tablespoons of the mixture to coat four 6-ounce steaks, chicken breast halves, or pieces of fish.

Stems of fresh or dried herbs placed on the coals or rack (always on the rack in gas grills) add flavor to foods cooked under a cover. Soak them for 30 minutes before using.

Note: To substitute dried herbs for fresh, lessen quantities by one-half to two-thirds.

HERB-CRUSTED ROASTED FISH STEAKS WITH PLUM SALSA

Makes 4 servings

Borrowing the herb crust customary for rack of lamb and then roasting quickly at high heat yields a moist, evenly cooked, rich-tasting fish. Fresh coriander (cilantro), sorrel, or basil could readily substitute for the watercress in the salsa.

For the plum salsa

1½ cups finely chopped pitted red plums

1 medium-size avocado, peeled, pitted, and finely chopped

¾ cup finely chopped orange or red bell pepper

¼ cup finely chopped red onion

2 tablespoons minced watercress

1 tablespoon red wine vinegar

1 tablespoon virgin or extra virgin olive oil

For the fish

1 tablespoon virgin or extra virgin olive oil

1 cup fresh whole wheat bread crumbs

2 tablespoons minced shallot

1 garlic clove, minced

⅓ cup Dijon mustard

2 tablespoons minced fresh fennel leaves

2 tablespoons white sesame seeds

Four 6-ounce halibut, tuna, or swordfish steaks about 1 inch thick, rinsed and patted dry

Prepare the salsa at least 1 hour before serving to allow the flavors to blend. Combine all the salsa ingredients in a nonreactive bowl, cover, and chill.

Preheat the oven to 450°F and coat a baking sheet with a light brushing of olive oil or nonstick cooking spray.

In a small nonstick skillet, heat the oil over medium heat. Add the bread crumbs, shallot, and garlic and cook, stirring constantly, until bread crumbs are golden, about 2 minutes. Remove from the heat and set aside.

In a small bowl, combine the mustard, fennel, and sesame seeds. Spread some of this mixture on each side of the fish steaks, then coat each side with some of the bread-crumb mixture, pressing it slightly. Place the coated fish steaks on the baking sheet and roast in the oven until the fish is opaque, 10 to 15 minutes. Serve warm with the plum salsa.

STIR-FRIED SCALLOPS WITH ASPARAGUS AND SPRING HERBS

Makes 4 servings

Crunchy asparagus teams up with succulent scallops, green onions, garlic chives, and arugula in a spicy ginger sauce. Shoyu is a Japanese soy sauce that is lower in salt; it is available at health food stores.

1 tablespoon cornstarch

½ cup vegetable stock (see page 36) or canned broth

2 tablespoons sherry vinegar

2 tablespoons shoyu

1 teaspoon minced fresh ginger

½ teaspoon hot red pepper sauce

2 teaspoons vegetable oil, preferably canola

2 tablespoons minced fresh garlic chives

*10 scallions, both white and green parts,
sliced diagonally into 1-inch lengths*

1 cup shredded arugula leaves

*1 pound asparagus, trimmed and sliced diagonally
into 1-inch lengths*

1¼ pounds sea scallops, rinsed and dried

*¼ cup coarsely chopped toasted pecans,
(see page 69)*

In a small bowl, whisk together the cornstarch, stock, vinegar, shoyu, ginger, and hot pepper sauce. Set aside.

Heat 1 teaspoon of the oil in a wok or large nonstick skillet over medium-high heat. When hot, add the garlic chives, scallions, arugula, and asparagus and stir-fry until the asparagus is crisp-tender, about 3 minutes. Remove from the wok.

Add the other teaspoon of oil and the scallops and stir-fry for 1 minute. Stir in the stock mixture and cook until thickened, 1 minute. Add the asparagus mixture and the pecans and cook for 1 minute to heat through. Serve immediately with rice or another grain.

LEMON THYME SHRIMP GRILL

Makes 4 servings

Few herbs are as versatile as lemon thyme. It combines all the wonderful qualities of thyme, which seems to have the ability to make ingredients pull together, with an intense bouquet of citrus. The plants themselves are lovely 8-inch mounds of tiny dark green leaves.

For the shrimp and vegetables

¼ cup virgin or extra virgin olive oil

3 tablespoons fresh lemon juice

1 tablespoon minced fresh lemon thyme leaves

1 pound large shrimp, peeled and deveined, with tails left on

*Assorted vegetables for grilling, cut into 1-inch pieces:
red, yellow, and green bell peppers, green or
yellow summer squash, pear or Italian tomatoes,
eggplant, or blanched pearl onions*

For the sweet onion–lemon thyme relish

2 tablespoons virgin or extra virgin olive oil

*1 pound sweet yellow or red onions, cut in half lengthwise
and thinly sliced (about 3 cups)*

2 tablespoons minced fresh lemon thyme leaves

3 tablespoons red wine vinegar

½ teaspoon hot red pepper sauce

½ teaspoon honey

To make the marinade, combine the olive oil, lemon juice, and lemon thyme in a glass measuring cup.

Using metal or wooden skewers that have been soaked in water for 30 minutes, thread 4 or 5 shrimp on a skewer, repeating until all the shrimp are used. Thread the vegetables onto additional skewers. Place the skewered shrimp and vegetables in a shallow nonreactive dish and pour the marinade over them. Marinate for 30 minutes.

To prepare the relish, heat the oil in a large nonstick

skillet over medium heat. Add the onions and cook, stirring, until transluscent, 15 to 20 minutes. Stir in the lemon thyme, vinegar, hot pepper sauce, and honey and cook, stirring, until the onions are soft and glazed, 5 to 8 minutes. The relish can be prepared 2 days ahead and chilled. Serve warm or at room temperature.

Prepare the grill, coating the grilling rack with nonstick cooking spray. If you're using briquettes or wood, let the fire burn down to hot coals. Place the skewers on the grill and cook for about 3 minutes per side. Serve with the relish.

CRAB CAKES WITH DILL SAUCE

Makes 4 servings

Crab cakes are meant to be simple and straightforward, focusing on the crab, which should be the best possible.

Those who decry the brevity of dill before it goes to seed are now assuaged. With the availability of 'Fernleaf' dill in 1992, dill lovers obtained 18-inch-tall plants that produce an abundance of dark blue-green leaves. Use this in ornamental or container plantings as well as in the herb garden.

For the dill sauce

⅓ cup nonfat or low-fat plain yogurt

3 tablespoons reduced-calorie or nonfat mayonnaise

¼ cup minced fresh dill

½ teaspoon Dijon mustard

Dash of hot red pepper sauce

For the crab cakes

3 tablespoons whole wheat saltine cracker crumbs

3 tablespoons reduced-calorie or low-fat mayonnaise

1 teaspoon Dijon mustard

1 tablespoon drained capers

¼ cup minced fresh Italian (flat-leaf) parsley leaves

¼ teaspoon salt

¼ teaspoon freshly ground black pepper

Pinch of ground cayenne pepper

1 pound fresh lump crabmeat, picked over
for cartilage and shell

1 tablespoon virgin or extra virgin olive oil

To prepare the sauce, combine the ingredients in a bowl.

To prepare the crab cakes, combine all the ingredients except the crabmeat and oil in a large bowl. Add the crab, tossing lightly to combine. Shape into 8 cakes.

Heat the oil in a nonstick skillet over medium heat. Cook the crab cakes until golden, about 3 minutes per side. Serve warm with the dill sauce.

HOT CHINESE BEEF WITH ANISE HYSSOP AND ORANGE

Makes 4 to 6 servings

Anise hyssop is a guileless summer-blooming perennial that has blended effortlessly into my cottage-style garden. Yes, it does readily go to seed and scatter about, which is precisely what I want in this type of garden, but if seedlings are ever unwanted, they are easily pulled up. The reward is billowing plants sending up innumerable spires of lilac-colored flowers in summer and fall.

Renee Shepherd's Special Treasure Chinese Beef provided the initial inspiration for this recipe. Serve with rice or vermicelli and steamed broccoli or carrots with minced garlic chives.

Shoyu is a Japanese soy sauce that is lower in salt; it is available at health food stores.

½ cup minced fresh anise hyssop flowers and leaves

⅓ cup fresh orange juice

2 tablespoons sherry vinegar

2 tablespoons shoyu

1 tablespoon honey

2 teaspoons grated orange zest

½ teaspoon hot red pepper flakes

1 pound flank, skirt, or top round steak, sliced diagonally into ¼-inch-thick slices

2 teaspoons cornstarch

2 teaspoons vegetable oil, preferably canola

1 teaspoon hot pepper sesame oil

Make a marinade by combining the anise hyssop, orange juice, vinegar, shoyu, honey, zest, and pepper flakes in a nonreactive dish. Add the beef to the marinade, stir to coat, cover, and let stand for 30 minutes at room temperature.

Remove the meat from the marinade and stir the cornstarch into the reserved marinade. Heat a wok or large nonstick skillet over medium-high heat and add the vegetable oil by pouring it in a circle near the rim. When the oil is hot, add the meat and fry, stirring constantly until cooked through, about 3 to 5 minutes. Add the reserved marinade and cook until the sauce is thickened, continuing to stir, about 2 minutes. Drizzle with the sesame oil, stir, and serve immediately.

GRILLED STEAK WITH CHIMICHURRI SAUCE

Makes 2½ cups

Growing up on a farm and continuing to raise beef cattle as an adult has made me value lean, tender beef produced without chemicals. Eating beef in moderation and preferably locally produced with a minimum of grain feeding means it doesn't have to be nutritionally or politically incorrect.

Not for the timid, chimichurri sauce is Argentinian in origin, where it is also used with grilled or roasted fish and chicken as well as with vegetables and sandwiches. Prepare it ahead of time, allowing the flavors to marry. It keeps for several weeks in the refrigerator.

For the chimichurri sauce

2 cups fresh parsley leaves

¼ cup fresh coriander (cilantro) leaves

¼ cup fresh spearmint leaves

¼ cup fresh tarragon or Mexican marigold mint leaves

1 tablespoon fresh oregano leaves

1 tablespoon fresh thyme leaves

*2 fresh bay leaves, midribs removed
(omit if only dry is available)*

4 garlic cloves

1 medium-size yellow onion

3 fresh jalapeño peppers, stems removed and seeded

¾ cup red or white wine vinegar or herb vinegar of choice

¾ cup virgin or extra virgin olive oil

Juice of 1 lemon

1 teaspoon freshly ground black pepper

½ teaspoon salt

For the steak

Steaks of choice, such as T-bone, tenderloin, porterhouse, or strip, about 6 ounces per person, cut 1 inch thick

Mince all the herbs and finely chop the garlic, onion, and jalapeños by hand or in a food processor. Combine with the vinegar, oil, lemon juice, pepper, and salt, either whisking together or pulsing several times in the food processor, being careful not to overprocess.

To grill the steak, bring beef to room temperature for fast, even cooking. Coat the grilling rack with nonstick cooking spray. If using briquettes or wood, let the fire burn down to hot coals. To seal in the juices, sear the steaks for 30 seconds on each side, then return to the original side. For rare, cook for about 3 minutes per side, for medium 5 minutes per side, and for well done 7 minutes per side. Remove from the grill and let rest for 5 minutes. Serve with the chimichurri sauce.

LAMB STEW WITH DILL AND CARAWAY

Makes 4 servings

From the heritage of the Romanians, Bulgarians, and Hungarians living along the Danube come elements of this shepherd's stew embellished with the aromatic seeds of caraway and dill.

Serve it with boiled new potatoes or egg noodles, black bread, and a marinated carrot salad.

2 tablespoons vegetable oil, preferably canola

1¼ pounds lean boneless lamb, cut into ½- by 2-inch strips

1 cup chopped yellow onions

1 garlic clove, minced

2 teaspoons sweet Hungarian paprika

2 tablespoons minced fresh dill

1 teaspoon caraway seeds

½ teaspoon dill seeds

1 teaspoon minced fresh marjoram leaves

1 bay leaf

½ teaspoon salt

½ cup water

¼ cup dry white wine

⅓ cup light sour cream

In a large saucepan or skillet with a lid, heat the oil over medium-high heat. Add the lamb and brown well on all sides. Remove and set aside. If necessary, pour off all but 2 tablespoons of pan drippings.

Add the onions and garlic and cook, stirring occasionally, until transluscent, about 5 minutes. Stir in the paprika, minced dill, caraway and dill seeds, marjoram, bay leaf, and salt. Return the lamb and any juices to the pan. Stir in the water and wine. Bring to a boil, cover, reduce the heat, and simmer until the lamb is tender, about 45 minutes. Uncover the pot, remove the bay leaf, turn up the heat, and cook until almost all the liquid is evaporated, about 3 to 5 minutes. Remove from the heat and stir in the sour cream. Return to low heat and cook just until heated through, never allowing it to boil. Serve immediately.

ROAST PORK LOIN WITH HERBS AND GLAZED APPLES

Makes 6 servings

From the early days of our republic, eating "high on the hog" has been a goal. Today it takes on a meaning besides affluence, as the leanest cut of pork is the tenderloin from along the back. This cut has only about the same amount of fat, cholesterol, and calories as skinless chicken breast, a significant change from only several decades ago.

With the apple accompaniment and serving this dish with a steamed vegetable like kale or snap beans and a whole grain such as brown rice or bulgur, you'll have a healthy taste of hog heaven.

Shoyu is a Japanese soy sauce that is lower in salt; it is available at health food stores.

2 tablespoons balsamic vinegar

2 tablespoons dry sherry

1 tablespoon virgin or extra virgin olive oil

1 tablespoon shoyu

1 tablespoon cracked black peppercorns

Two 3-inch fresh rosemary sprigs

Two 3-inch fresh marjoram sprigs

Two 3-inch fresh thyme sprigs

2 garlic cloves, minced

Two ⅔-pound pork tenderloins, trimmed of fat and membrane

Salt to taste

2 tablespoons vegetable oil, preferably canola

2 tablespoons unsalted butter or margarine

4 Gala, Golden Delicious, or other cooking apples, cored and cut into ¼-inch-thick rings

One 3-inch fresh sage sprig

¼ cup bourbon

2 tablespoons honey

Combine the vinegar, sherry, olive oil, shoyu, peppercorns, rosemary, marjoram, thyme, and garlic in a shallow nonreactive baking dish. Place the pork in the marinade, turning to coat, then cover with plastic wrap. Place in the refrigerator for several hours, turning several times. Remove from the refrigerator 20 minutes before cooking to bring to room temperature.

Preheat the oven to 425°F. Heat the vegetable oil in a large skillet over medium heat. Lift the pork from the marinade and brown on all sides, about 2 minutes per side. Place the pork in a nonreactive roasting pan and pour the marinade over it. Sprinkle lightly with salt and roast until the internal temperature reaches 150°F, about 20 minutes.

Meanwhile, melt the butter in the skillet over medium-high heat. Add the apples and sage and cook until the apples begin to turn golden, about 5 minutes, turning over occasionally. Add the bourbon and honey and continue cooking until the rings are almost translucent, another 10 minutes. Remove the sage.

Place the pork on a serving platter and surround it with the apple rings. To serve, cut the pork into 1-inch-thick slices.

TURKEY SCALOPPINE WITH BASIL-CUCUMBER SAUCE

Makes 4 servings

Turkey breast cutlets may be the ultimate quick-change artist. One day they offer me a simple sandwich, and on another an elegant piccata sauced with lemon. The essential requirement for preparing these with the least possible fat is always to use a nonstick skillet. Serve this incarnation of turkey scaloppine with broiled tomatoes topped with bread crumbs and steamed chard sprinkled with toasted walnuts.

¼ cup unbleached all-purpose flour

¼ cup freshly grated Parmesan cheese

Salt and freshly ground black pepper to taste

1¼ pounds turkey cutlets

1 tablespoon unsalted butter or margarine

2 tablespoons virgin or extra virgin olive oil

3 tablespoons minced fresh basil leaves

1 teaspoon minced fresh thyme leaves

¾ pound cucumbers, peeled, quartered lengthwise, seeded, and cut into ½-inch pieces (about 1 large)

½ cup dry white wine

2 teaspoons Dijon mustard

¼ cup light sour cream

1 tablespoon minced fresh chives or parsley leaves

Mix the flour and cheese with salt and pepper. Lightly dust the cutlets on both sides with the mixture. Heat the butter and 1 tablespoon of the oil in a large nonstick skillet over medium-high heat. Add the cutlets and cook until both sides are golden, turning once, about 2 minutes per side. Transfer to a warm platter.

Add the other tablespoon of oil to the skillet. Stir in the basil, thyme, and cucumbers and cook for 3 minutes, stirring constantly. Add the wine, raise the heat to high, and cook until reduced by half, stirring occasionally, about 3 to 5 minutes. Remove from stove and blend in the mustard and sour cream, then pour the sauce over the turkey. Sprinkle with chives and serve immediately.

CHICKEN THIGHS GLAZED WITH ORANGE-THYME-CUMIN SAUCE

Makes 4 servings

If chicken thighs weren't so inexpensive, we would probably be impressed by their dark, moist, deep flavor. I like to serve this chicken with grilled polenta slices with ground coriander and a spinach salad.

Shoyu is a Japanese soy sauce that is lower in salt; it is available at health food stores.

½ cup dry white wine, vegetable stock (see page 36), or water

¼ cup sherry vinegar

¼ cup fresh orange juice

2 tablespoons fresh lime juice

3 tablespoons shoyu

2 tablespoons minced fresh thyme leaves

1 tablespoon minced fresh garlic chives or 1 garlic clove, minced

1 tablespoon honey

1 teaspoon minced fresh ginger

1 teaspoon ground cumin

1 fresh jalapeño pepper, cored, seeded, and minced

8 chicken thighs, skinned

In a large nonstick skillet, combine all the ingredients except the chicken. Over medium-high heat, bring the mixture to a boil, then add the chicken. Reduce the heat to low, cover, and simmer for 15 minutes. Remove the cover, turn the chicken pieces over, raise the heat to medium, and cook until the liquid is evaporated and the chicken is glazed, about 15 minutes.

Free-range chickens yield wholesome and delicious eggs that combine with herbs for mouth-watering omelets.

A field of corn awaits the autumn harvest.

LILLY'S GRILLED CILANTRO-LIME CHICKEN WITH VEGETABLES

Makes 4 to 6 servings

In a relatively short period of time Lilly's has become a Louisville, Kentucky, landmark for its innovative food. Restaurateur Kathy Cary, along with dinner chef Giulia Isetti, continually explore ways to reinterpret dishes. This marinade relies on the bold flavor of fresh coriander (cilantro) and other mainly Southeast Asian ingredients, but the vegetables served with it are an unusual combination of down-home American with south-of-the-border and Chinese.

Shoyu is a Japanese soy sauce that is lower in salt; it is available at health food stores.

½ cup shoyu

1 tablespoon stone-ground mustard

Juice of 2 limes

2½ tablespoons rice wine vinegar

¼ cup chopped fresh coriander (cilantro) leaves

Hot red pepper sauce to taste

2 tablespoons sesame oil

½ cup virgin or extra virgin olive oil

3 whole chicken breasts, boned, skinned, and cut in half

1 medium-size yellow onion, chopped

1 medium-size red bell pepper, cored, seeded, and cut into thin strips

1 medium-size yellow bell pepper, cored, seeded, and cut into thin strips

1 cup cubed peeled jicama

1 medium-size head bok choy, sliced

3 ears white corn, with corn cut off cobs, or 1½ cups corn kernels

4 tablespoons (½ stick) cold unsalted butter or margarine

In a nonreactive bowl, whisk together the shoyu, mustard, lime juice, vinegar, coriander leaves, hot pepper sauce, and oils. Place the chicken breasts in a nonreactive dish and pour half the marinade over the top. Cover and chill for 8 hours.

Prepare the grill, coating the grilling rack with nonstick cooking spray. If you're using briquettes or wood, let the fire burn down to hot coals. Wipe the marinade from the chicken. Grill the chicken breasts, basting with reserved marinade on both sides until cooked through, about 5 minutes on each side. Cover and set aside.

Heat all the remaining marinade in a large nonstick skillet over medium-high heat. Add the onions and peppers and cook for 5 minutes. Add the jicama, bok choy, and corn and cook for 4 minutes more. Turn off the heat and whisk in the butter a tablespoon at a time.

Put the vegetables and sauce on a platter. Top with the chicken and serve.

TOFU STIR-FRIED WITH CHINESE GREENS

Makes 4 servings

One of my most prized possession is a bird's-eye maple tofu press handmade by a very special friend. He and I would spend the hours making tofu on a wood stove discussing life, love, work, food, and plants, not necessarily in that order. Such bucolic days are gone, and so is he, but my pleasure in eating tofu remains. Whether simply marinated and roasted as my friend Ilze taught me, as an "eggless" salad heaped in sandwiches, or as ivory cubes floating in miso soup, well-made tofu is a joy.

Where once it was an oddity, now almost every grocery produce department has tofu. For most cooking, I buy very firm tofu made from organic soybeans. After the sealed packages are open, tofu can be kept for several days in the refrigerator if it is stored in water that is changed daily.

Still rare are the many different Asian greens. Unless you live near a market that offers them, you'll either have to grow your own or rely solely on Chinese cabbage and bok choy, also known as pak choi, or American greens like spinach, kale, and chard. You'll be missing out on aromatic edible chrysanthemum, beautifully lacy mizuna, or the radiating rosettes of tatsoi.

Some of the best sources of Asian vegetable seed include Johnny's Selected Seeds, Nichols Garden Nursery, Vermont Bean Seed Company, and Pinetree Garden Seeds. See the Sources section (page 150) for addresses.

Shoyu is a Japanese soy sauce that is lower in salt; it is available at health food stores.

For the Asian marinade

¼ cup shoyu

¼ cup rice wine vinegar

2 tablespoons dry sherry

1 teaspoon grated horseradish

1 tablespoon grated fresh ginger

2 garlic cloves, minced

1 teaspoon sesame oil

1 tablespoon honey

1 small fresh jalapeño or other hot pepper, cored, seeded, and minced

2 tablespoons minced fresh coriander (cilantro) leaves

2 tablespoons minced fresh basil leaves

1 teaspoon minced fresh mint leaves

For the stir-fry

1 pound firm or extra-firm tofu, cut into ½-inch cubes

2 tablespoons sesame, peanut, or other vegetable oil

1 large yellow onion, cut in half vertically, and thinly sliced

4 to 6 cups coarsely chopped mixed greens

1 teaspoon cornstarch

Combine all the marinade ingredients in a nonreactive bowl or dish. Add the tofu cubes and let stand for at least 15 minutes.

Drain the tofu from the marinade, reserving it. Place a wok or large nonstick skillet over high heat and drizzle 1 tablespoon of the oil around the rim of the pan. Add the tofu cubes and cook, stirring constantly, until golden, 3 to 4 minutes. Remove and set aside.

Add the other tablespoon of oil and the onion. Stir-fry for 2 minutes. Add the greens and cook until wilted and tender, 3 to 5 minutes. Time will vary depending on the type and age of the greens. Stir the cornstarch into the reserved marinade and add to the wok. Cook until thickened, another few minutes. Stir in the reserved tofu. Serve immediately with hot rice.

TORTELLINI WITH SUN-DRIED TOMATOES, SQUASH, AND NASTURTIUMS

Makes 4 servings

As incredibly flavorful as it is beautiful, this amalgam distills the essence of glorious summer days and a garden that feeds both body and spirit. For a perfect picnic, add a crisp wine, crusty bread, and loving friends or family.

18 fresh nasturtium flowers

2 scallions, both white and green parts, finely sliced

1 teaspoon minced fresh thyme leaves

1 teaspoon minced fresh savory leaves

1 teaspoon minced fresh parsley leaves

1 teaspoon minced fresh chives

1 minced garlic clove

Salt and freshly ground black pepper to taste

2 tablespoons virgin or extra virgin olive oil

½ cup oven- or sun-dried tomatoes

Boiling water

1 pound fresh tortellini

8 baby scallop squash with their blossoms

8 baby zucchini squash with their blossoms

⅓ cup vegetable stock (see page 36), dry white wine, or water

Fresh nasturtium flowers and leaves

Remove the green bases from the nasturtium flowers and chop. Blend these with the scallions, thyme, savory, parsley, garlic, chives, salt, pepper, and olive oil. Let stand for 30 minutes.

Soften the dried tomatoes by covering them with boiling water and letting sit for 2 minutes. Drain, slice thinly crosswise, and set aside.

Cook the tortellini in a large pot of boiling water until they rise to the surface. Drain and toss with half of the herb mixture.

Slice the squash and blossoms thinly crosswise. In a nonstick skillet, heat the other half of the herb mixture over medium heat and cook the tomatoes and squash for 3 minutes, stirring occasionally. Add the stock and squash blossoms and simmer over low heat for 2 minutes. Toss the vegetables with the pasta and serve immediately, garnishing with fresh nasturtium flowers and leaves.

PASTA WITH RADICCHIO, MUSHROOMS, AND HERBS

Makes 4 servings

Like a piece of stunningly wrought sculpture, radicchio, with its sensuously undulating curves and folds of contrasting pearlescent white and deep, dark wine, invites contemplation. Usually a salad ingredient, radicchio may also be sautéed, baked, or grilled. Here it is combined with another beautiful plant, oyster mushrooms, and the clarity of fresh chives, thyme, and marjoram. For such a straightforward dish, use only the best olive oil and aged Parmigiano-Reggiano.

¾ pound farfalle or penne
¼ cup virgin or extra virgin olive oil
½ pound radicchio, thinly sliced
2 garlic cloves, minced
½ pound fresh oyster mushrooms, thinly sliced
½ cup freshly grated Parmesan cheese
2 tablespoons minced fresh Italian (flat-leaf) parsley leaves
1 tablespoon minced fresh chives
2 teaspoons minced fresh thyme leaves
2 teaspoons minced fresh marjoram leaves
Salt and freshly ground black pepper to taste

Bring a large pot of salted water to a boil over high heat. Add the pasta and cook according to package instructions until al dente.

Meanwhile, heat the oil in a large nonstick skillet over medium heat. Add the radicchio and garlic and cook for 1 minute, then add the mushrooms and cook until tender and wilted, another 2 to 3 minutes, stirring frequently.

Drain the pasta and put it in a large bowl. Add the radicchio mixture, Parmesan cheese, and herbs. Toss thoroughly. Season with salt and pepper. Serve immediately.

An autumn-bowered creek and old water-powered gristmill remind us of the labor required to grind the grain for pasta.

Salads,
Vegetables,
and
Side Dishes

Summer Squash Salad with Parsley and Nasturtium
Braised Turnips with Rosemary and Thyme
Snap Beans with Garlic, Fennel, and Ginger
Broccoli with Sesame, Garlic, Ginger, and Tarragon

Vegetables, salads, and grains have finally gotten their chance at center stage. The health benefits of their complex carbohydrates, vitamins, and minerals are touted in newspapers and magazines. Where once we relied on meat and potatoes with some overcooked green beans on the side, now the best restaurants showcase vegetables and their counterparts. Vegetables, greens, and grains unknown 20 years ago are commonplace today in groceries and farmer's markets.

For growing your own, seed catalogs offer dozens of varieties from around the world, from past centuries, and from the latest of the breeder's art. Even if you have just a small garden plot or a terrace with a few containers, search out and try varieties that have exceptional flavor or vitamins. Many of the seed companies listed in the sources section (page 150) are noted for their efforts to carry the best varieties for home gardens. Don't settle for the ordinary.

Whether homegrown or market-bought, an entire meal of vegetables—steamed, grilled, roasted, sautéed, or baked in parchment—accompanied by a salad combining sweet and bitter greens and a grain (such as one of the rices, barley, couscous, or quinoa) is food for the gods.

Of course all of these foods take splendidly to herbs that highlight flavors without adding calories. Where once we may have thought only of potatoes and parsley or peas and mint, now there are infinite combinations.

For instance, try chives with peas; tarragon with asparagus; dill with beets, potatoes, or summer squash; thyme with almost anything, but especially the winter vegetables; rosemary with potatoes, onions, or green beans; sage with winter squash, onions, or polenta; garlic with greens, broccoli, or mushrooms; and basil with eggplant, summer squash, potatoes, or carrots.

Toss some minced fresh herbs in with salads, too. Herb flowers are great for both garnishing and flavoring. Try those of nasturtium, hyssop, savory, thyme, basil, rosemary, or dill.

Note: To substitute dried herbs for fresh, lessen quantities by one-half to two-thirds.

SNAP BEANS WITH GARLIC, FENNEL, AND GINGER

Makes 4 servings

Beans are one of those vegetables that you may think boring if you know them only canned or frozen. What you can grow in the garden or sometimes find at farmer's markets are dozens and dozens of different varieties in a lot of different shapes, sizes, and colors.

Some of the best herbs to use with green beans are savory, thyme, basil, dill, lovage, mint, parsley, garlic, and tarragon as well as the ginger and fennel featured in this recipe.

Hazelnut oil is available at many health food stores and gourmet food shops.

½ cup whole hazelnuts

1 pound fresh snap beans, ends removed,
cut diagonally into 2-inch pieces

1 tablespoon hazelnut oil

1 tablespoon unsalted butter or margarine

1 tablespoon minced fennel leaves

1 teaspoon minced fresh ginger

1 garlic clove, minced

Salt and freshly ground black pepper to taste

Preheat the oven to 350°F. Place the nuts in a baking pan large enough to hold them in a single layer. Bake for 10 minutes, stirring once. Remove the nuts from the oven and wrap in a kitchen towel, rubbing them to remove the skins. Cool and chop finely.

Blanch the green beans in a pot of boiling salted water for about 3 minutes. Drain, rinse in cold water, and pat dry with a towel.

In a large skillet, heat the oil and butter over medium heat. Add the fennel, ginger, and garlic and cook, stirring, until soft, about 2 minutes. Add the beans and hazelnuts and cook until hot, another 3 minutes, stirring occasionally. Season with salt and pepper and serve.

FRESH BABY SHELL BEANS WITH GARLIC, PARSLEY, AND SAVORY

Makes 4 servings

Baby shell beans, whether flageolets, limas, cranberry, or favas, are a delicacy that few people know about. Clutch them to your heart if you see them in stores. Fortunately, they are easily grown in home gardens. Flageolets, favas, and American shell beans are better adapted to areas with long, cool springs; limas do best in hot southern climates. Any of these are benefited by the traditional combination of beans with tomatoes and the garlic, parsley, and savory.

The secret to their nutty-tasting, tender goodness is harvesting them just as the beans are well formed and beginning to separate from the pod. They freeze well and are also excellent with vinaigrette or in soups.

2 tablespoons virgin or extra virgin olive oil

1 garlic clove, minced

½ cup thinly sliced scallions, both white and green parts

1½ cups baby shell beans

1 cup peeled and seeded (see page 31), then chopped, ripe tomatoes (about ½ pound)

2 tablespoons minced fresh parsley leaves

1 tablespoon minced fresh savory leaves

Salt and freshly ground black pepper to taste

In a small skillet, heat the oil over medium-high heat. Add the garlic and scallions and cook, stirring, until translucent, about 3 minutes. Stir in the beans, tomatoes, parsley, and savory and reduce the heat to medium. Cook until the beans are tender, 6 to 8 minutes. The cooking time will vary depending on the maturity of the beans, sometimes taking as long as 20 minutes. Season with salt and pepper and serve hot.

BROCCOLI WITH SESAME, GARLIC, GINGER, AND TARRAGON

Makes 4 to 6 servings

Broccoli has developed mass appeal in the United States only since the 1920s. High in vitamins A and C, iron, calcium, and potassium, these little green trees are very low in calories. The sesame oils called for can be found at Asian markets and health food stores. Shoyu is a Japanese soy sauce that is lower in salt; it is also available at Asian markets and health food stores.

1 medium-size red bell pepper

2 tablespoons white sesame seeds

1 pound fresh broccoli, cut into medium-size florets

2 tablespoons sesame oil

1 teaspoon hot pepper sesame oil

1 garlic clove, sliced

1 teaspoon minced fresh ginger

One 15-ounce can baby corn, drained and soaked in ice water for 30 minutes

½ cup scallions, both white and green parts, thinly sliced

1 teaspoon minced fresh tarragon leaves

2 tablespoons minced fresh garlic chives

2 tablespoons rice wine vinegar

2 teaspoons shoyu

Preheat oven to 400°F. Place the bell pepper in a shallow baking pan and roast, uncovered, until its skin is brown and blistered, about 20 minutes. Alternatively, place the pepper under a broiler, turning until all sides are charred. Let cool. Peel the skin away, cut in half, discard the seeds and stems, and cut into strips.

Toast the sesame seeds in a dry skillet over medium heat just until golden, about 2 minutes.

Place the broccoli in a steamer pot over an inch of boiling water, cover, and steam until tender but still crisp, 3 to 5 minutes. Rinse under cold water and drain well.

Meanwhile, heat the oils in a large skillet over medium heat, add the garlic and ginger, cook for 2 minutes, stirring, then remove and discard. Add the steamed broccoli, roasted peppers, baby corn, scallions, tarragon, garlic chives, vinegar, shoyu, and toasted sesame seeds. Cook just until everything has warmed, about 3 to 5 minutes. Serve warm, at room temperature, or chilled.

BRAISED ONIONS WITH TARRAGON AND WINE

Makes 4 servings

Slightly astringent, yet with a soft anise-like flavor, tarragon lends an intriguing quality to these pink-tinted onions. Mexican marigold mint has a more pronounced anise taste, and it grows more readily in the South. Vidalia-type onions are planted in the fall in mild-winter areas for spring harvest, while the sweet Spanish are spring-planted for fall harvest.

2 tablespoons unsalted butter or margarine

2 tablespoons virgin or extra virgin olive oil

4 large sweet or mild onions, cut into ½-inch slices (about 1⅓ pounds)

2 tablespoons tarragon vinegar

⅓ cup blush or rosé wine

2 teaspoons minced fresh tarragon or Mexican marigold mint leaves

Salt and freshly ground black pepper to taste

Heat the butter and oil in a large nonstick skillet over medium-high heat. Add the onions and cook, stirring, until beginning to soften, about 2 minutes. Add the vinegar and wine, reduce the heat to low, and simmer until very soft, about 10 to 12 minutes. Stir in the tarragon and cook for 3 minutes. Season with salt and pepper and serve immediately.

BRAISED TURNIPS WITH ROSEMARY AND THYME

Makes 4 servings

Unless one is close to the land and nature's cycles, it's easy to forget that even winter brings us plants that are at their peak of flavor. How easy it is to overlook such supposedly humble vegetables as turnips, rutabagas, and parsnips. Yet these easily grown plants yield wonderfully flavored dishes that are inextricably linked with fall and winter's substantial meals.

1 pound small turnips and/or rutabagas, peeled and diced (about 3 cups)

½ pound carrots, thinly sliced diagonally (about 1½ cups)

1 medium-size yellow onion, thinly sliced

1 garlic clove, minced

1 tablespoon minced fresh rosemary leaves

1 teaspoon minced fresh thyme leaves

4 tablespoons (½ stick) unsalted butter or margarine, cut into ¼-inch slices

½ cup dry red wine

Salt and freshly ground black pepper to taste

Preheat the oven to 350°F. In an ovenproof dish, combine the turnips, carrots, onion, garlic, rosemary, and thyme. Dot the butter over the vegetables. Pour the wine over the top. Cover and bake until the vegetables are tender, about 45 minutes. Season with salt and pepper and serve hot.

ROASTED POTATOES WITH HERBS

Makes 4 servings

While not as low-calorie as steaming, roasting vegetables with herbs yields such incredible flavor that the light coating of oil can be readily justified. Cooking at high temperatures in the oven gives the essense of grilling without the hassles, and meals can be prepared in a very short time.

Potatoes with rosemary are first in line for this technique, but eggplant, carrots, summer squash, asparagus, leeks, peppers, fennel, baby sweet potatoes, baby turnips, and green beans are some of the others that taste sublime this way. Besides rosemary, try basil, cilantro, dill, garlic chives, hyssop, lovage, marjoram, oregano, parsley, sage, savory, or thyme with the different vegetables. Sesame or peanut oil can be substituted for the olive oil.

Freshly dug new potatoes, each about the size of a golfball, are one of gardening's pleasures. Try growing 'Cherries Jubilee', with its unusual pink color, as well as 'Alaska Red', 'Bison', or 'Rhinered'.

1½ pounds small new red potatoes, quartered (about 16)

1 tablespoon minced fresh rosemary leaves

1 tablespoon virgin or extra virgin olive oil

Salt and freshly ground black pepper to taste

Preheat the oven to 400°F. In a baking pan, combine the potatoes, rosemary, and oil. Stir until the potatoes are well coated with the oil. Bake, stirring occasionally, until the potatoes are golden and tender, 20 to 30 minutes. Season with salt and pepper and serve immediately.

CARROTS GLAZED WITH MINT, MAPLE, AND BOURBON

Makes 4 servings

Bourbon and mint are natural partners, at least in Kentucky in May, and the combination works with carrots as well, especially when paired with all-American maple syrup. Sometimes I use another whiskey, wine, or brandy or orange, lemon, or lime juice. Of course honey can substitute for the maple syrup. Besides mint, I like to use basil, chives, dill, ginger, mint, nutmeg, oregano, parsley, sage, savory, or thyme with carrots.

Use whole round or cylindrical baby carrots or larger carrots sliced on the diagonal, julienned, or carved into 2-inch ovals. For maximum nutrition, try carrot varieties with extra-high vitamin A content such as 'Juwarot' or 'A-Plus'.

1 pound carrots, trimmed as desired

2 tablespoons water

2 tablespoons bourbon

2 tablespoons unsalted butter or margarine

1 tablespoon pure maple syrup

¼ cup minced fresh mint leaves

Salt and freshly ground black pepper

Combine the carrots, water, and bourbon in a large nonstick skillet over medium heat. Cover and cook, stirring occasionally, until the carrots are tender when pierced, about 5 minutes depending on size. Add the butter, maple syrup, and mint and stir. Continue to cook, uncovered, until the liquid has evaporated and the carrots are glazed, about 2 to 3 minutes. Season with salt and pepper and serve immediately.

73

PICKLED CARROT SALAD WITH HOT PEPPERS AND DILL

Makes 4 servings

These pickled carrots pack a nice wallop. Obviously they go well with Southwest-inspired menus, but they are also delightful served with soup and sandwiches for lunch or as part of an antipasto tray. The "coolness" of the dill provides an interesting undertone.

If you're impatient or haven't had much success growing carrots, let the quickly growing round or small "baby" carrots inspire you. Try 'Mokum' for early spring gardens, 'Minicor' for crisp, sweet 4-inch carrots, and 'Thumbelina' for 1- to 1 1/2-inch round roots. For continued harvests, make new plantings every 2 weeks from early to late spring and again in late summer.

1 pound fresh baby carrots

½ cup dry white wine

¼ cup plain or flavored white wine vinegar

1 garlic clove, peeled

1 fresh jalapeño or other hot pepper

Two 5-inch fresh dill sprigs

One 3-inch cinnamon stick

½ teaspoon yellow or brown mustard seeds

1 teaspoon celery seeds

2 tablespoons honey

Red leaf lettuce

Dill, nasturtiums, apple trees, and squash, overleaf, coexist ebulliently in this garden.

In a medium-size saucepan, combine all the ingredients except the lettuce. Bring to a boil over medium heat, then reduce the heat to low and simmer until the carrots are tender, about 15 minutes. Chill the carrots in the marinade for at least 6 hours or overnight. Drain and arrange the carrots on the lettuce leaves. Strain the marinade and drizzle over the carrots.

76

Produce like these carrots at a farmer's market, inspires shoppers to cook to their heart's content.

SUMMER VEGETABLE AND BREAD SALAD

Makes 6 servings

Found in various guises in the Mediterranean region, this rustic salad can be a meal in a bowl, especially with cubes of feta or mozzarella. Use the freshest, most flavorful of ingredients and flat-leaf Italian parsley if at all possible. Make the effort, too, to search out coriander (cilantro) varieties that are bred to maximize foliage rather than quickly going to seed.

⅓ cup fresh lemon juice or 2 tablespoons basil-red wine vinegar (see page 124)

¼ cup virgin or extra virgin olive oil

2 garlic cloves, minced

Salt and freshly ground black pepper to taste

3 or 4 medium-size ripe tomatoes, cut into ½-inch cubes

1 medium-size cucumber, peeled, seeded, and sliced or cubed

1 medium-size green, yellow, red, or purple bell pepper, cored, seeded, and cut into thin strips

½ cup thinly sliced scallions, both white and green parts

4 to 6 romaine or leaf lettuce leaves, finely sliced

⅓ cup chopped fresh parsley leaves

⅓ cup chopped fresh coriander (cilantro) leaves

¼ cup chopped fresh spearmint leaves

2 tablespoons chopped fresh basil leaves

2 tablespoons chopped fresh oregano leaves

⅓ cup pitted and chopped black Niçoise or Kalamata olives

8 ounces feta or fresh mozzarella, cubed (optional)

2 whole wheat pita rounds, toasted and cut into wedges, or 2 cups toasted Italian whole wheat bread cubes

In a small bowl, whisk together the lemon juice, oil, garlic, salt, and pepper.

In a large bowl, combine the remaining ingredients except the bread. Pour the dressing over the top, toss, and let marinate for 30 minutes at room temperature. Add the bread immediately before serving.

SUMMER VEGETABLES WITH CINNAMON BASIL

Makes 4 servings

Adding cinnamon basil to this American translation of the Provençal mélange of summer's bounty may seem like a sacrilege, but one taste will persuade otherwise. Suggested by Ellen Ogden of the seed company The Cook's Garden, Londonderry, Vermont, the basil's spicy perfume serves to intensify the flavors of the vegetables.

Young, recently picked eggplant is a revelation, with little of the bitterness often associated with eggplant and no peeling, salting, and draining necessary. Besides the usual dark purple, eggplants in shades of white, pink, and lavender are gaining notice, as are varieties with fruits of various shapes and sizes. A French hybrid, 'Prelane', has long cylindrical fruit that never get bitter and hold their shape well with cooking. No matter which of the dozens of varieties you choose, be sure to pick eggplant while still shiny, cutting, not tearing, the fruits from the plant, and harvesting regularly to keep the handsome plants producing all summer.

2 tablespoons virgin or extra virgin olive oil

2 medium-size yellow onions, chopped

2 garlic cloves, minced

1 pound eggplant, cut into 1-inch cubes and tossed with 2 tablespoons fresh lemon juice

1 medium-size red or yellow bell pepper, cored, seeded, and cut into ½-inch-wide strips

1 teaspoon minced fresh thyme leaves, preferably lemon thyme

½ pound zucchini or other summer squash, cut into 1-inch cubes

1 pound tomatoes, peeled and seeded (see page 31), then cut into 1-inch cubes

2 tablespoons minced fresh cinnamon basil leaves

2 tablespoons minced fresh basil leaves

¼ cup minced fresh parsley leaves

Salt and freshly ground black pepper to taste

Heat the oil in a large skillet over medium heat. Add the onion and garlic and cook, stirring, until the onion is translucent, 6 to 8 minutes. Add the eggplant, bell pepper, and thyme and continue cooking, stirring frequently, until the vegetables are tender but still crisp, about 10 minutes. Add the zucchini, tomatoes, basil, and parsley and cook, continuing to stir, until the squash is tender, about 5 minutes. Season with salt and pepper. Serve warm or at room temperature.

WHITE BEAN AND HERB SALAD

Makes 6 servings

Mediterranean cooks have taken more than one native American vegetable to their bosom, making it seem almost their own. This influence extends to the ubiquitous bean. Dried white beans, especially, are transformed by the Italian touch with herbs, lemon, and olive oil. Nutritious and high in fiber, beans make a substantial salad for summertime luncheons or a side dish to hearty stews or vegetable casseroles year-round. The character of this salad is readily altered by adding different meats. For instance, I like to add smoked duck sausage, grilled chicken or tuna, or even caviar. Different kinds of white beans can be used, including navy and cannellini, but Great Northerns cook up the best.

1 cup dried white beans, picked over

1 small yellow onion, chopped

2 garlic cloves, minced

One 3-inch fresh rosemary sprig or 1 teaspoon dried rosemary

One 3-inch fresh sage sprig or 1 teaspoon dried sage

2 fresh lovage leaves or 1 celery rib, chopped

1 bay leaf

1 cup peeled and seeded (see page 31), then chopped, tomato (about ½ pound)

1 medium-size red or green bell pepper, cored, seeded, and finely chopped

½ cup minced fresh herb leaves: basil, chives, dill, marjoram, mint, oregano, parsley, savory, tarragon, thyme, or any combination

⅓ cup lemon juice or white wine vinegar

⅓ cup virgin or extra virgin olive oil

1 tablespoon Dijon mustard

Salt and freshly ground black pepper to taste

Put the beans in a large heavy saucepan, cover with cold water, and soak overnight. Drain and combine with enough cold water to cover by 2 inches, the onion, garlic, rosemary, sage, lovage, and bay. Cover and simmer over low heat until the beans are tender, about 2 hours. Remove from heat. Gently stir in the tomato, bell pepper, and herbs. In a small bowl, whisk together the lemon juice, oil, mustard, salt, and pepper. Stir into the beans. Allow the flavors to marry for at least an hour before serving. Chill if the salad is not to be served right away, but it is best at room temperature.

SPICED CUCUMBERS AND CARROTS WITH GINGER, GARLIC CHIVES, AND CINNAMON BASIL

Makes 4 to 6 servings

One of the oldest of cultivated crops, cucumbers are incredibly easy to grow, and a number of varieties are nonbitter and "burpless." These include the lemon cucumber, Middle Eastern types like 'Hylares' or 'Amira', standard types like 'Burpless Bush' or 'Sweet Success', and the long types that must be grown on a trellis like 'Early Perfection', 'Suyo Long', or 'Armenian'.

If you can't grow your own cucumbers, search out a farmer's market during the summer or get the long type grown in greenhouses that are available year-round. None of these will be waxed as are most standard cucumbers offered in groceries.

The Asian-inspired flavors combined here complement the refreshing taste of the cucumbers. This is a light appetizer that would admirably start a rich meal of lamb or pork. Because it doesn't contain dairy products or mayonnaise, it also makes a great picnic or party food.

Shoyu is a Japanese soy sauce that is lower in salt; it is available at health food stores.

3 cups (about 2, depending on type) thinly sliced cucumber

1 cup 2-inch-long carrot matchsticks (about ⅓ pound)

3 scallions, both white and green parts, finely sliced

1 tablespoon rice wine vinegar

1 tablespoon fresh lime juice

2 tablespoons sesame oil

½ teaspoon honey

1 teaspoon shoyu

1 tablespoon minced fresh garlic chives or 1 garlic clove, minced

1 tablespoon minced fresh cinnamon basil leaves

½ teaspoon minced fresh ginger

½ teaspoon hot red pepper flakes or sauce

Put the cucumbers in a bowl and sprinkle lightly with salt. Toss and let stand for 30 minutes. Drain, chill for 30 minutes, and drain again. Combine the cucumbers with the carrots and scallions. Whisk the vinegar, lime juice, and sesame oil together. Add the remaining ingredients and mix well. Pour this dressing over the vegetables. Marinate in the refrigerator for several hours or overnight. Serve chilled or at room temperature.

STEPHEN LEE'S WILTED SPINACH SALAD WITH MARINATED YOGURT CHEESE

Makes 4 servings

Nowhere is it written that spinach salad must contain egg and bacon, yet that is almost invariably how it's served. Cooking instructor Stephen Lee developed this version with hot and spicy flavors mingling with the sweetness of the mint and tang of the the yogurt cheese.

Be sure to use an exhaust fan when warming the spices because the fumes can be caustic.

1 cup fresh mint leaves

1 tablespoon salt

¼ cup fresh lime juice

1 teaspoon curry powder

1 tablespoon sesame oil

2 cups homemade yogurt cheese (see page 23)

1 tablespoon cumin seeds

1 teaspoon ground coriander

½ teaspoon ground cayenne pepper

¼ cup virgin or extra virgin olive oil

1 pound fresh spinach, well washed, stems removed, and coarsely shredded

1 medium-size cucumber, peeled, seeded, and diced

Pita rounds cut into wedges

One hour before serving, combine the mint, salt, lime juice, curry powder, and 1 tablespoon oil in a food processor or blender. Pour over the yogurt cheese in a bowl and let marinate at room temperature.

In a heavy skillet over medium-high heat, combine the cumin seeds, coriander, and cayenne. Stirring, warm them for 2 minutes, then add the 1/4 cup olive oil and heat for another minute or two.

Have the spinach and cucumbers ready in a bowl and pour the excess mint marinade over the top, then the hot spiced oil. Toss and serve immediately, with a large dollop of the cheese for each serving and pita wedges.

SUMMER SQUASH SALAD WITH PARSLEY AND NASTURTIUM

Makes 4 to 6 servings

Even in years when I don't have much time to garden, I grow over a half dozen different kinds of summer squash. Besides at least one variety each of the green French, Italian, and Middle Eastern zucchini, I include the beautifully shaped scallop, or patty pan, squash, the straight-neck yellow squash, and the crook-neck yellow. When space is an issue, the pale yellow oval-shaped 'Sun Drops' and crook-neck 'Butter Swan' are my choices. For nutrition, flavor, and versatility, 'Kuta' stands out. With almost 100 percent more phosphorus and calcium than other summer squash, 'Kuta' also contains above-average amounts of vitamins A and C and potassium. Most unusual, though, is that the fruits can be used when young as summer squash or left to mature into hard-shelled winter squash.

6 small (about 1½ pounds) summer squash, coarsely grated or cut into 2-inch matchsticks
½ cup minced fresh Italian (flat-leaf) parsley leaves
½ cup minced fresh nasturtium leaves
½ cup minced fresh nasturtium flowers
3 tablespoons champagne vinegar, preferably herb-flavored
⅓ cup virgin or extra virgin olive oil

1 tablespoon minced fresh basil leaves
1 teaspoon Dijon mustard
Salt and freshly ground black pepper to taste
Tomato slices
Fresh nasturtium flowers

In a mixing bowl, combine the squash, parsley, and nasturtium leaves and flowers. In a small bowl, whisk together the vinegar, oil, basil, mustard, salt, and pepper. Pour the dressing over the zucchini mixture and toss. Serve on a bed of tomato slices and garnish with nasturtium flowers.

COLD SESAME NOODLES WITH VEGETABLES AND CILANTRO

Makes 4 to 6 servings

———

There are innumerable ways to make sesame noodles, but including vegetables makes this a wholesome main-course vegetarian salad. It's also an excellent accompaniment to a simply grilled fish or chicken entree. Or serve smaller portions as an appetizer. I like to take it to pitch-in dinner parties, too. Pasta made from spelt grain—available at many health food stores — is organically produced, has a higher protein content than regular pasta, and is well tolerated by people with wheat allergies.

Shoyu is a Japanese soy sauce that is lower in salt, it is available at health food stores.

For the hot sauce

2 tablespoons sesame oil

1 teaspoon hot pepper sesame oil

2 garlic cloves, peeled

2 tablespoons minced fresh ginger

2 scallions, both white and green parts, thinly sliced

½ cup coarsely chopped cilantro leaves

¼ cup smooth peanut butter

¼ cup shoyu

¼ cup rice wine vinegar

1 teaspoon honey

To finish the dish

1 pound spelt or other vermicelli, cooked al dente, drained, tossed with 1 tablespoon vegetable oil, (preferably canola), and chilled

1 medium-size cucumber, peeled, seeded, and cut into 2-inch matchsticks

1 medium-size zucchini, cut into 2-inch matchsticks

1 cup shredded carrots

1 cup peeled and seeded (see page 31), then chopped, ripe tomato (about ½ pound)

6 scallions, both white and green parts, thinly sliced

¼ cup white sesame seeds

Combine the hot sauce ingredients in a food processor or blender and blend until smooth.

Toast the sesame seeds in a dry skillet over medium heat just until golden, about 3 minutes.

To serve, place the noodles in a large bowl or on a platter, pour the sauce over them, and toss. Arrange the vegetables on top, then sprinkle with the toasted sesame seeds. Serve cold or at room temperature.

GREEN RISOTTO

Makes 4 servings

———

The delicate and creamy texture of a risotto made with Arborio rice cannot be duplicated using any other form of rice. Grown only in Italy, the short, round, starchy grains are also exquisitely flavored. (Interestingly, pearl barley does make an exceptional risotto.) With a salubrious amalgam of whatever fragrant herbs that whim and garden yield, risotto is an elegant partner to a meal or even the meal itself, perhaps with the addition of only a salad. Fresh vegetables and fish or seafood, either fresh or smoked, can be added to the risotto.

Don't be afraid to mix what seems like an unholy alliance of herbs; most often they'll form an angelic coalescence. Other types of rice and other grains are also good with a quantity of herbs as used here.

2 tablespoons unsalted butter or margarine

2 tablespoons virgin or extra virgin olive oil

¼ cup minced shallot

1 small garlic clove, minced

1½ cups Arborio rice

1 quart vegetable stock (see page 36), or canned vegetable broth, heated

½ cup dry white wine

½ cup minced fresh herbs, including any combination of arugula, basil, borage, burnet, calendula petals, chervil, chives, coriander (cilantro), dill, fennel, garlic chives, hyssop, lovage, marjoram, Mexican marigold mint, nasturtium, oregano, parsley, rosemary, sage, savory, sorrel, tarragon, thyme, or watercress

½ cup freshly grated Parmesan cheese

Salt and freshly ground black pepper to taste

Heat the butter and oil in a large heavy saucepan over low heat. Add the shallots and garlic and cook until translucent, about 2 minutes. Add the rice, stirring to coat thoroughly with the butter and oil.

Stir in 1 cup of the stock and cook until the liquid is absorbed, 6 to 8 minutes. With a large fork, loosen the rice from the sides and bottom of the pan. Add another cup of stock and cook until absorbed, about 5 minutes. Stir the rice again with the fork. Repeat twice more, adding the stock, letting it cook until absorbed, then loosening with the fork. Finally, add the wine and herbs, cooking until the liquid is absorbed, about 5 minutes. The rice should be tender. If not, add a little warm water and cook until the rice is tender but still firm.

Stir in the cheese, heating until it is melted. Season with salt and pepper and serve immediately.

SOLSTICE BARLEY SALAD WITH CITRUS-HERB DRESSING

Makes 6 to 8 servings

Tess Krebs, deli chef of the Rainbow Blossom, a health food store in Louisville, Kentucky, got me started with her Thai and Indian combinations. This version relies on garden munificence at its peak.

Hulled, or whole grain, barley, available from health food stores, has the greatest nutritional value, but the more widely seen pearl barley still has plenty of protein, B vitamins, and phosphorus, as well as potassium, and it cooks much faster.

For the salad

3 cups water

1 teaspoon salt

1 cup pearl barley

1 medium-size cucumber, peeled, seeded, and diced

8 scallions, both white and green parts, thinly sliced

1½ cups zucchini or summer squash, diced (about ½ pound)

½ cup thinly sliced radishes

1 medium-size green bell pepper, cored, seeded, and cut into 2-inch matchsticks

½ cup shelled green peas or snap beans cut into 1-inch lengths, blanched for 2 minutes (optional)

12 arugula leaves, torn into pieces

4 fresh sorrel leaves, torn into pieces

2 tablespoons minced fresh lemon basil leaves

Calendula petals

Borage flowers

For the citrus-herb dressing

1 garlic clove, minced

1 teaspoon minced fresh ginger

1 teaspoon minced fresh lemon thyme leaves

1 tablespoon minced fresh tarragon leaves

1 tablespoon tarragon vinegar

1 tablespoon fresh lime juice

¼ cup virgin or extra virgin olive oil

Salt and freshly ground black pepper to taste

Bring the water to a boil over high heat in a medium-size saucepan. Add the salt and barley, reduce the heat to low, and simmer, uncovered, until just tender, 35 to 40 minutes. Drain and chill well.

Place the remaining salad ingredients except the flowers in a large bowl and toss well.

Make the dressing by whisking all its ingredients together in a small bowl. Pour the dressing over the barley-vegetable mixture and mix well. Garnish with calendula petals and borage flowers.

Breads,
Muffins, and
Crackers

Spiral Herb Bread
Whole Wheat Baking Mix Muffins
Apricot Bread with Poppy Seed
Sage-Onion Corn Bread
Herb Goat Cheese Rounds
Oatmeal Scones with Flowers and Sweet Herbs
Carrot and Coriander Muffins
Angel Biscuits with Herbs
Stephen Lee's Zucchini-Pesto Muffins
Lemon Herb Tea Bread
Dill-Onion Bread

One of the great treats of my childhood was to spend an afternoon settled down with a freshly made bread, herb butter, and a good book. For that matter, it still is a wonderful way to relax. Only now instead of adding herbs to the butter, I put them directly into the dough. The results are no less satisfying and a lot healthier.

For most of my baking I use some mixture of whole wheat and unbleached all-purpose flours from organically grown wheat. Depending on the texture desired, I may mix them half and half or two-thirds to one-third. If you prefer to use only white or unbleached all-purpose flour, substitute that in the recipes. When making yeast breads, I use at least some bread flour made from hard winter wheat. This requires extra liquid and kneading but produces a lighter loaf. Whole grain flours tend to turn rancid quickly, so store them in tightly closed bags in the freezer.

Should it come as any surprise that biscuits, scones, pancakes, muffins, quick breads, yeast breads, sourdough items, pizza, focaccia, and crackers all benefit from herbs? Although fresh herbs have the strongest scent, their flavor is milder and brighter than when dried. A warm mellowness is the trademark of dried herbs. My preference is for a pronounced herb flavor, so I often use about 3 tablespoons of fresh herbs for every 2 cups of flour called for in a recipe.

Besides adding herbs to the batter or dough, try brushing the tops of biscuits, breads, or crackers either before or after baking with an herb-infused oil. A more subtle way of introducing scent and flavor is to spread branches of herbs like rosemary hyssop, fennel, or thyme on the baking sheet and then bake rounded loaves on top.

The sweeter herbs, like angelica, sweet cicely, cinnamon basil, mint, rose geranium, lemon balm, lavender, anise hyssop, bergamot, violets, and roses lend a wonderful air to breads made with a sweet batter. Don't forget about using herb seeds and flowers as well as the leaves.

Note: To substitute dried herbs for fresh, lessen quantities by one-half to two-thirds.

ANGEL BISCUITS WITH HERBS

Makes twenty-four 2-inch biscuits

Light as an angel's kiss, these biscuits are a specialty of the South. Many southern cooks swear that biscuits should be made only with White Lily flour, but try them even if you don't have access to this silken stuff. Biscuits such as these will never be mistaken for health food, but many a hardy soul with great longevity has been nurtured by them.

My choices of herbs for biscuits vary with when and how they will be served. Crushed fennel seeds or minced sage or thyme leaves complement sausage gravy. Edible flowers like bergamot, nasturtium, pineapple sage, rose, or anise hyssop as well as sweet herb leaves like rose geranium, mint, or cinnamon basil lend the biscuits to afternoon tea, especially when served with homemade herb jellies and jams. Fresh chive, oregano, or thyme blossoms make for a festive brunch biscuit. Biscuits with fresh dill leaves would complement salmon cakes or smoked fish.

One ¼-ounce envelope active dry yeast

2 tablespoons warm water (110° to 115°F)

¾ cup buttermilk, at room temperature

*¼ cup minced fresh herb leaves or flowers or
2 tablespoons crushed herb seeds*

2½ cups unbleached all-purpose flour

2 tablespoons sugar

1½ teaspoons baking powder

½ teaspoon baking soda

½ teaspoon salt

*½ cup (1 stick) cold unsalted butter or margarine,
cut into 8 pieces, or ½ cup solid vegetable shortening*

In a small bowl, dissolve the yeast in the warm water and let stand for 10 minutes. It should foam; if not start again with fresh yeast. Stir in the buttermilk and herbs.

Sift the flour, sugar, baking powder, baking soda, and salt together. Using a pastry cutter blender, 2 knives, or a food processor, cut in the butter until the mixture resembles coarse crumbs. Add the yeast mixture to the flour mixture, stirring or processing just until a dough is formed. Turn out on a floured surface and knead until the dough is soft and smooth, about 5 minutes. Biscuits can be made at once or the dough refrigerated, tightly covered, for up to 3 days.

To bake, preheat the oven to 400°F. Roll the dough out 1/2 inch thick on a lightly floured surface. Cut with a 2-inch biscuit cutter, cutting straight down, never twisting. Dough scraps can be rerolled. Place the biscuits 2 inches apart on a greased or parchment-covered baking sheet or one coated with a nonstick cooking spray. Cover with a clean, dry towel and let stand in a warm place for 30 minutes, until doubled. Bake until golden brown, 10 to 15 minutes. Remove from the sheet and serve warm.

WHOLE WHEAT
BAKING MIX

Makes 6 cups

Homemade baking mix gives you the advantage of using more nutritious ingredients, including whole wheat flour and mono-unsaturated vegetable oil rather than the white flour and solid shortening used in commercial mixes. Use this mix to make biscuits, muffins, and pancakes, adding whatever herbs or edible flowers you prefer. Soy flour and brewer's yeast can be found at health food stores and some supermarkets.

3 cups whole wheat all-purpose flour

1½ cups unbleached all-purpose flour

½ cup soy flour

1 cup instant nonfat dry milk

1 tablespoon baking soda

¼ cup wheat germ

2 tablespoons brewer's yeast

1 cup vegetable oil, preferably canola

Combine the flours, dry milk, baking soda, wheat germ, and brewer's yeast in a mixing bowl or food processor. Add the oil and mix, using a pastry blender, electric mixer, or food processor, until it resembles coarse crumbs. Place in an airtight container and store in the refrigerator for up to 3 months.

For biscuits, combine 2 cups baking mix with 1/3 cup buttermilk and 2 tablespoons minced herbs or 1 tablespoon crushed herb seeds, stirring until the dough leaves the sides of the bowl. Turn onto a lightly floured board and knead 5 times. Roll the dough out 3/4 inch thick and cut into circles with a floured 2-inch biscuit cutter. Place 1 inch apart on an ungreased baking sheet, and bake in a preheated 400°F oven until golden brown, 10 to 12 minutes. Makes six to eight 2-inch biscuits.

For muffins, put 2 3/4 cups baking mix into a large bowl and stir in 3 tablespoons of minced herbs or 1 tablespoon crushed herb seeds. In another bowl, whisk together 1/4 cup honey, 2 large eggs, and 1 cup buttermilk. Stir just until the dry ingredients are moistened. Spoon into a greased and floured 12-cup muffin pan, filling them full. Bake in a preheated 400°F oven until golden brown, about 20 minutes. Makes 12 muffins.

To make pancakes, combine 3/4 cup buttermilk, 1 large egg, 1 cup baking mix, and 1 tablespoon minced herbs or 1 teaspoon crushed herb seeds. Cook on a lightly greased hot griddle. Turn the pancakes over when bubbles form on the surface. Makes four 5-inch pancakes. Use batter to make 2-inch pancakes to use as a base for appetizers, topped with such tidbits as smoked fish, grilled chicken, or cucumber slices.

OATMEAL SCONES
WITH FLOWERS AND
SWEET HERBS

Makes 12 scones

Scones originated in Scotland as triangle-shaped quick breads made with oats and cooked on a griddle, evolving today into sweetened biscuits made with flour and baked. Savor these warm from the oven at breakfast with butter and jelly, at lunch with a fresh fruit salad, or for tea with jam and Devonshire cream.

Sweet herbs and flowers complement scones of any sort. Use either diced fresh or candied angelica stems, the minced leaves of sweet cicely, lemon balm, lemon verbena, mint, or rose geranium, or the flowers of anise hyssop, bergamot, hyssop, lavender, or roses.

1 cup buttermilk

1 cup rolled oats

½ cup dried cherries, dried cranberries, or dried currants

1 cup unbleached all-purpose flour

½ cup whole wheat all-purpose pastry flour

¼ cup sugar

1 teaspoon baking powder

¼ teaspoon salt

3 tablespoons minced fresh herb flowers or leaves

*6 tablespoons (¾ stick) unsalted cold butter or margarine,
cut into 6 pieces*

In a bowl, stir together the buttermilk, oats, and fruit. Cover and refrigerate at least 6 hours or overnight.

Preheat the oven to 400°F. Mix the flours, 3 tablespoons of the sugar, the baking powder, salt, and herbs together in another bowl. Cut in the butter with a pastry blender or 2 knives or process in a food processor until the mixture resembles coarse crumbs. Add the buttermilk mixture and stir or process just until a soft

dough forms that pulls away from the sides of the bowl.

Turn the dough out onto a lightly floured surface and knead 8 to 10 times. Cut the dough in half and form each piece into a ball. Pat or roll each ball into a circle 1/2 inch thick. Cut each circle into 6 wedges. Place the wedges 1/2 inch apart on an ungreased baking sheet. Sprinkle with the remaining sugar. Bake until golden brown, about 25 minutes. Serve warm.

BLUEBERRY-MINT PANCAKES

Makes eight 4-inch pancakes

With dozens of varieties readily available, almost all of which have robust growth, mint tends to find its way into unexpected places in my cooking. It goes well with most fruits and brings a sweetness to foods without adding sugar. I generally prefer spearmint for cooking, with 'Kentucky Colonel' and 'English' the two cultivars that are the staples in my garden.

½ cup yellow cornmeal

¼ cup minced fresh mint leaves

½ cup boiling water

½ cup unbleached all-purpose flour

½ cup whole wheat all-purpose flour

2 tablespoons sugar

2 teaspoons baking powder

½ teaspoon salt

1 large egg, beaten

*2 tablespoons unsalted butter or margarine,
melted and cooled*

1 cup skim milk

2 cups fresh or thawed frozen blueberries

Put the cornmeal and mint in a bowl and pour the boiling water over them, stirring well. Add the flours, the remaining ingredients except the berries, and stir until blended.

Heat the griddle over medium-high heat, lightly oiling it when hot or using nonstick spray. Pour 1/4 cup batter onto the griddle for each pancake. When bubbles are breaking the surface, sprinkle on 1/4 cup of the blueberries, gently pressing them into the pancake with a turner. Turn the pancake over and finish cooking for about another minute, or until the bottoms are lightly browned. Serve these hot with juice-sweetened blueberry syrup.

REFRIGERATOR MUFFINS WITH HERBS

Makes 36 muffins

For those times when you want to eat rather than cook, this batter produces a healthy, high-fiber muffin with minimal preparation. You can bake as few or as many as you want, making them ideal for either an individual breakfast or an impromptu brunch. The batter is prepared far in advance, the herbs added just before baking.

2 cups buttermilk

1½ cups whole-bran cereal

½ cup rolled oats

½ cup vegetable oil, preferably canola

4 large egg whites

½ cup honey

1 cup whole wheat all-purpose flour

½ cup unbleached all-purpose flour

2½ teaspoons baking soda

½ teaspoon salt

1 cup raisins, dried cranberries, or dried cherries

1 cup chopped nuts

For each muffin: 1 teaspoon minced fresh herb leaves or 1/2 teaspoon crushed herb seeds.

In a large bowl, pour the buttermilk over the bran cereal and oats and stir. Let stand for 10 minutes. Stir in the oil, egg whites, and honey. Combine the remaining ingredients in another bowl. Add to the buttermilk mixture, stirring just until blended. You can store the batter in a tightly covered container in the refrigerator for up to 2 weeks.

To prepare, preheat the oven to 400°F. Grease a muffin pan or coat with a nonstick cooking spray. Remove as much batter as desired and add minced herbs. Fill the muffin cups full. Bake until the muffins are golden brown and spring back when touched lightly, 15 to 20 minutes. Cool on a wire rack for 10 minutes before removing from the pan, then serve at once.

STEPHEN LEE'S ZUCCHINI-PESTO MUFFINS

Makes 12 muffins

The prolific zucchini meets America's passion for pesto and mania for muffins in this delectable accompaniment to a brunch or perhaps a lunch of fresh green salad or soup. The only change I made to Louisville, Kentucky, cooking instructor Stephen Lee's heart-healthy recipe was to use some whole wheat flour. Any type of summer squash may be used, including the flavorful Lebanese-type zucchini like 'Zahra' or 'Ghada'.

1½ cups unbleached all-purpose flour

1 cup whole wheat pastry flour

4 teaspoons baking powder

½ teaspoon salt

1 large egg

2 large egg whites

⅔ cup skim milk

⅓ cup virgin or extra virgin olive oil

1 cup shredded zucchini

3 tablespoons minced fresh basil leaves

1 teaspoon minced garlic

⅓ cup freshly grated Romano cheese

½ cup pine nuts

Preheat the oven to 425°F. Grease a 12-cup muffin pan or coat with a nonstick cooking spray. Sift the flours, baking powder, and salt into a large mixing bowl. In another bowl, whisk together the egg, egg whites, milk, and oil until well blended. Add the egg mixture to the flour mixture and beat just until blended. Stir in the zucchini, basil, garlic, cheese, and pine nuts. Fill each muffin cup full of batter. Bake until the muffins are golden brown and spring back when touched lightly, about 20 minutes. Cool on a wire rack for 10 minutes before removing from the pan, then serve at once.

Herb gardens such as this one yield both sweet and savory herbs to use in breads for every occasion and time of day.

CARROT AND CORIANDER MUFFINS

Makes 12 muffins

Ground coriander, with its flavor suggesting sage and caraway with a hint of lemon, has been used in cooking for so long that mention of it was made in early Sanskrit writings. Carrots are probably the most readily available

of all organically grown produce, so I buy my carrots when I can't have them from the garden.

1 cup unbleached all-purpose flour

1 cup whole wheat pastry flour

1 tablespoon baking powder

½ teaspoon baking soda

¼ teaspoon salt

1 teaspoon ground coriander

½ cup chopped pecans

½ cup golden raisins

1 large egg, beaten

3 tablespoons vegetable oil, preferably canola

¼ cup honey

½ cup skim milk

½ cup nonfat or low-fat plain yogurt

1 cup grated carrots (about 1/3 pound)

Preheat the oven to 375°F. Grease a 12-cup muffin pan or coat with a nonstick cooking spray. In a large bowl, combine flours, baking powder, baking soda, salt, coriander, nuts, and raisins. In another bowl, combine the egg, oil, honey, milk, yogurt, and carrots. Add the carrot mixture to the flour mixture, stirring just until blended. Spoon the batter into the muffin cups, filling each full. Bake until the muffins are golden brown and spring back when touched lightly, about 25 minutes. Cool on a wire rack for 10 minutes before removing from the pan, then serve at once.

LEMON HERB TEA BREAD

Makes one 8- by 4-inch loaf

A break for hot tea and a bit of something sweet is a time-honored custom that brings comforting contentment. Moist and tart-sweet, this tea bread is the perfect foil to a pot of Earl Grey tea, which is scented with the oil of bergamot oranges. The three lemon herbs used—lemon balm, lemon verbena, and lemon thyme—are all vigorous,

easily grown plants. Use all three as flavoring for this or other breads and desserts as well as with fish or poultry. This recipe may also be made into three 6- by 3-inch loaves that are perfect for gifts.

For the tea bread

⅔ cup skim milk

1 tablespoon minced fresh lemon balm leaves

1 tablespoon minced fresh lemon thyme leaves

1 tablespoon minced fresh lemon verbena leaves

2 cups unbleached all-purpose flour

2 teaspoons baking powder

¼ teaspoon salt

6 tablespoons (¾ stick) unsalted butter or margarine, at room temperature

1 cup granulated sugar

2 large eggs

1 tablespoon grated lemon zest

For the lemon glaze

2 tablespoons fresh lemon juice

½ cup confectioners' sugar

A colorful parterre boasts a host of herbs.

Preheat the oven to 325°F. Grease a 4- by 8-inch loaf pan or coat with a nonstick cooking spray. In a small saucepan, combine the milk and minced herbs. Over low heat, bring just to a simmer, remove from the heat, and set aside to steep. Sift the flour, baking powder, and salt together into a bowl. In a large bowl, cream the butter, then gradually add the sugar, beating until light and fluffy. Beat in the eggs one at a time, beating well after each addition, then add the lemon zest. Add a third of the flour mixture and a third of the herbed milk, mixing just until blended. Repeat twice more. Pour the batter into the prepared pan and bake until golden brown and a toothpick inserted in the center of the bread comes out clean, about 50 minutes. Let cool on a wire rack for 10 minutes. Turn out onto a serving plate, keeping the top side up. Combine the lemon juice and confectioners' sugar. Prick the top of the loaf with a fork and pour the glaze over the bread. Cut into slices to serve. This will keep about 3 to 5 days in an airtight container.

RHUBARB–BLACK WALNUT BREAD WITH ANGELICA

Makes one 8- by 4-inch loaf

Rhubarb is a favorite plant of mine because of its versatility in both the garden and the kitchen. Grown among my perennial flowers, the large leaves and bright red stems add bold, exotic texture. A long-lived perennial requiring only minimal care, rhubarb has thick fleshy stems that are a good source of vitamins A and C as well as potassium. The first "fruit" of spring, rhubarb stems traditionally have their tartness offset by angelica, an herb with a natural sweetness. Sweet cicely has the same characteristic and may be substituted.

Rhubarb leaves are toxic and should never be eaten.

½ cup sugar

1 cup diced rhubarb stems

½ cup unbleached all-purpose flour

1 cup whole wheat pastry flour

1½ teaspoons baking powder

½ teaspoon baking soda

¼ teaspoon salt

1 large egg

¼ cup fresh orange juice

¼ cup vegetable oil, preferably canola

2 tablespoons minced fresh angelica leaves and stems or
1 tablespoon minced candied angelica stems

¾ cup chopped black walnuts

In a small bowl, sprinkle the sugar over the rhubarb and let sit for 1 hour, stirring occasionally.

Preheat the oven to 350°F and grease a 4- by 8-inch

loaf pan or coat with a nonstick cooking spray. Sift the flours, baking powder, baking soda, and salt together into a large bowl. In another bowl, whisk the egg with 1/4 cup of the juice from the steeped rhubarb, the orange juice,

vegetable oil, and angelica. Add the egg mixture to the flour mixture, stirring just enough to blend. Drain the rhubarb and fold it and the nuts into the batter. Pour the batter into the prepared pan and bake until a toothpick inserted in the center comes out clean, about 45 minutes.

Let cool on a wire rack for 10 minutes, then remove from pan. Cut into slices to serve. This will keep about 3 days in an airtight container.

APRICOT BREAD WITH POPPY SEED

Makes one 8- by 4-inch loaf

Closely related, apricots and almonds make a fragrant, flavorful pairing, with the poppy seeds adding an extra nuttiness to this colorful bread. Almonds are more nutritious than other nuts, being rich in protein, calcium, phosphorus, iron, and B vitamins, and the apricots provide vitamin A, potassium, and iron.

1 cup unbleached all-purpose flour

1 cup whole-wheat pastry flour

⅔ cup diced dried apricots

½ cup blanched, sliced almonds

2 teaspoons baking powder

½ teaspoon baking soda

½ teaspoon salt

2 tablespoons poppy seeds

1 cup skim milk

½ cup honey

¼ cup vegetable oil, preferably canola

1 teaspoon pure almond extract

1 large egg, beaten

1 tablespoon grated orange zest

Preheat the oven to 350°F. Grease or coat a 4- by 8-inch loaf pan with a nonstick cooking spray, then lightly flour it. In a large bowl, combine the flours, apricots, almonds, baking powder, baking soda, salt, and poppy seeds. In a small bowl, combine the remaining ingredients. Stir the milk mixture into the flour mixture just until blended. Pour the batter into the prepared pan and bake until a toothpick inserted in the center comes out clean, 45 to 50 minutes. Cool in the pan on a wire rack for 10 minutes, then remove from the pan and cool completely before slicing and serving. This will keep for about 5 days in an airtight container.

SAGE-ONION CORN BREAD

Makes one 8-inch square

Maize, or Indian corn, was the most important food in the early days of America, not so much as a vegetable but as the basic ingredient in porridges and breads. Most early travelers carried small bags of ground corn, which when mixed with water could be eaten raw or cooked over a fire, providing quick, nourishing sustenance. As the most traditional of American breads, corn bread has been given many names and forms, including johnnycake, journeycake, hoecake, spider cake, corn pone, Apache bread, scratch back, and ashcake. No matter what the name, corn bread is a very personal matter, with much contention as to sweet or plain, moist or dry. The southwestern influence on cooking has made corn bread with jalapeños and cheddar cheese a popular option. The version here matches a moist, plain cake with the camphorlike aroma and flavor of sage and the pungent sweetness of sautéed onions. Serve it with a salad for a meal in itself or pair it with stews, casseroles, or other savory dishes.

3 tablespoons vegetable oil, preferably canola

¾ cup chopped yellow onion

1 tablespoon minced fresh sage leaves

1¼ cups yellow cornmeal

1 cup unbleached all-purpose or whole wheat pastry flour

2 teaspoons baking powder

½ teaspoon baking soda

½ teaspoon salt

1 tablespoon honey

1 large egg

1¼ cups buttermilk

Preheat the oven to 400°F. Grease an 8-inch-square baking pan or coat with a nonstick cooking spray. Heat the oil in a small skillet over medium-high heat, add the onion and sage, and cook, stirring occasionally, until the onion is transparent, about 5 minutes.

While the onion is cooking, combine the cornmeal, flour, baking powder, baking soda, and salt in a large bowl. In a small bowl, combine the honey, egg, and buttermilk, whisking until thoroughly mixed. Stir the onion-sage mixture into the buttermilk mixture. Add the buttermilk mixture to the flour mixture, stirring just until combined. Pour the batter into the prepared pan and bake until golden brown and a toothpick inserted in the center comes out clean, 20 to 25 minutes. Let cool for 10 minutes before cutting and serving. This is best served fresh, but leftover corn bread is wonderful split and made into French toast.

DILL-ONION BREAD

Makes two 9- by 5-inch loaves

On a narrow, winding road outside of Midway, Kentucky, high on the banks of Elkhorn Creek, is a wonderful old building that houses Weisenberger Mills. The mill supplies flours and special mixes to stores and restaurants as well as local and mail-order customers. Phil

Weisenberger, the third of four generations of Weisenbergers to be involved in the mill, accumulates all manner of recipes using the flours they produce. This bread is a sturdy, stick-to-the-ribs kind that needs little more than some sliced ripe tomatoes and lightly cooked straight-from-the-garden vegetables to make a meal.

> 3 tablespoons plus 1 teaspoon honey
> ¼ cup warm water (110° to 115°F)
> Two ¼-ounce envelopes active dry yeast
> 2 cups low-fat large-curd cottage cheese
> 2 tablespoons grated yellow onion
> ¼ cup vegetable oil, preferably canola
> 4 teaspoons dill seeds
> 2 teaspoons salt
> ½ teaspoon baking soda
> 2 large eggs
> 4 to 4½ cups whole wheat all-purpose or bread flour

In a small bowl, stir 1 teaspoon of the honey into the warm water, then stir in the yeast. Set the yeast aside for 10 minutes.

In a large bowl, combine the cottage cheese, the remaining honey, the onion, oil, dill seeds, salt, and baking soda. Add the yeast mixture and stir. Then add the eggs and stir again. Add enough flour, 1 cup at a time, to make a stiff dough, beating well after each addition. Turn the dough out onto a lightly floured surface and knead until the dough is smooth and elastic, 8 to 10 minutes. If the dough seems too sticky, add a handful of flour.

Place in a greased bowl, turn once to coat the top, cover with a clean dry towel, and place in a warm spot to rise until doubled in bulk, about 1 hour. Punch down, knead gently for 1 or 2 minutes, and shape into 2 loaves. Place in greased 9- by 5-inch loaf pans or coat with nonstick spray. Cover and place in a warm spot to rise until doubled in bulk, about 45 minutes. Preheat the oven to 350°F. Bake until the loaves sound hollow when tapped, 40 to 50 minutes. Remove from pans and cool on wire racks.

SPIRAL HERB BREAD

Makes two 9- by 5-inch loaves

The beauty of the interior of a seashell is translated into this lovely bread. Breads, more than any other food, are adaptable to a wide range of herbs, and this bread particularly lends itself to experimentation. Sage or dill stands alone well. Scallions and parsley provide a base for combinations such as rosemary and oregano or marjoram and thyme. Oregano, garlic, and fennel combine well with cooked sausage. Any pesto can be used, too. Herbs and grated cheese make a rich, substantial filling. As Pogo said, "We are faced with insurmountable opportunity."

1 cup skim milk

1 cup water

*3 tablespoons vegetable oil, preferably canola,
plus extra for brushing*

1 tablespoon honey

1 teaspoon salt

Two ¼-ounce envelopes active dry yeast

4 cups unbleached all-purpose flour

2 cups whole wheat all-purpose flour

2 tablespoons unsalted butter

3 cups minced fresh herb leaves

Salt and freshly ground black pepper to taste

1 large egg

In a saucepan, combine the milk, water, oil, honey, and salt and heat until warm (110°F). Remove from the heat and stir in the yeast. Set aside in a warm place for 10 minutes, then pour into a large bowl. Stir in the unbleached flour, 1 cup at a time, making sure the batter is smooth. Add the whole wheat flour, 1 cup at a time, until a stiff dough that leaves the sides of the bowl is easily formed.

Turn the dough out onto a floured surface and knead until the dough is smooth and elastic, about 10 minutes. Add flour if the dough seems too sticky. Place in an oiled bowl, turning the dough to oil the surface. Cover with a clean, dry towel and let rise in a warm place until doubled in bulk, about 1 to 1 1/2 hours. Punch the dough down and let it rest for 10 minutes.

Heat the butter over medium heat in a large skillet and add the herbs, cooking just until they wilt. Season with salt and pepper. Let cool for 5 minutes. Beat the egg lightly and stir it into the herbs.

Divide the dough in half and roll each piece into a rectangle about 9 by 12 inches. Spread half of the herb mixture on each rectangle, leaving a 1-inch margin around the edges. Roll the dough up tightly lengthwise. Pinch the dough to seal and tuck the ends under. Place in greased 9- by 5-inch loaf pans or coat with nonstick spray, seam side down. Brush the tops with vegetable oil, cover, and let rise in a warm place until doubled in size, about 1 hour. Preheat the oven to 375°F. Bake until golden brown and hollow sounding when tapped, about 50 minutes. Remove the loaves from the pans and cool on a wire rack. If you can resist, wait to slice until thoroughly cool.

HERB GOAT CHEESE ROUNDS

Make about 72 rounds

Nothing could be easier, yet more elegant, than these little bites of piquant richness. Baked, they are wonderful tossed in a fresh green salad, garnishing a creamed soup, accompanying a savory dip, or eaten just as is. Consider using almost any savory herb alone or in combination.

1 cup unbleached all-purpose flour

4 tablespoons (½ stick) cold unsalted butter or margarine, cut into 4 pieces

8 ounces fresh goat cheese, crumbled

¼ cup nonfat or low-fat plain yogurt

2 tablespoons minced fresh herb leaves

½ teaspoon salt

½ teaspoon freshly ground black pepper

1 large egg white

½ cup freshly grated Parmesan cheese

Combine all the ingredients, except the egg white and Parmesan cheese, in a bowl or food processor and mix or process just until a smooth dough is formed. Form the mixture into a log 1 inch in diameter. Wrap in wax paper or plastic wrap and chill for 1 hour. Preheat oven to 375°F. Cut the log into 1/4-inch-thick slices. Place on a lightly greased or parchment-covered baking sheet or one coated with a nonstick coating spray and prick the tops with a fork. Lightly beat the egg white and use a pastry brush to coat the rounds, then sprinkle with the Parmesan cheese. Bake until light golden brown, 15 to 20 minutes. Cool and store in an airtight container for up to several weeks.

The worn wooden shelves in a kitchen house, overleaf, tell of holding food and dishes for centuries.

A weathered barn door, left, returns us to the time when cooks raised or grew many of their ingredients.

HERB CRACKERS

Makes 72 crackers

Making homemade crackers in this day and age may seem more than slightly anachronistic, but the results are quite toothsome. Sesame seeds are traditional in crackers, but explore other options, using just one kind of herb or seed as well as the infinite combinations possible.

1½ cups unbleached all-purpose flour

½ cup whole wheat all-purpose flour

1 teaspoon baking soda

1 teaspoon baking powder

½ teaspoon salt

½ teaspoon dry mustard

3 tablespoons minced fresh herb leaves or whole seeds

1 teaspoon freshly grated or prepared horseradish

½ cup (1 stick) cold unsalted butter or margarine, cut into 8 pieces

1 large egg

¼ cup buttermilk

Combine the flours, baking soda, baking powder, salt, mustard, herbs, and horseradish in a mixing bowl or in a food processor bowl. Add the butter to the flour mixture and mix until pea-size pieces form. Add the egg and mix just until blended. Add the buttermilk and mix just until the dough starts to form a ball.

Turn the dough out onto a lightly floured board and knead for a few minutes. Divide the dough into 2 parts, wrap in wax paper or plastic wrap, and chill in the refrigerator for 1 hour.

Preheat the oven to 350°F. Working with one piece at a time, roll the dough out about 1/8 inch thick, flouring the board as necessary. Cut into rounds, squares, or other shapes using a small biscuit or cookie cutter or a sharp knife. Place on ungreased baking sheets and bake until golden, 10 to 12 minutes. Remove from the pans and cool, then store in tightly covered containers for several weeks.

Desserts

Of all my cooking, using herbs in desserts has brought me the greatest pleasure. It can come as such a surprise to discover how well herbs pair with sweets. Fruits, particularly, take on a new dimension with herbs, whether in pies, crisps, cobblers, or compotes. A simple dessert of fresh or dried fruit poached in wine and herbs can make an elegant finale to a meal.

The obvious first choices among the herbs to use in desserts are those with a sweetness to them. Angelica and sweet cicely are favored because their use means less sugar is needed. Other dessert herbs are anise, anise hyssop, cinnamon and anise basils, bergamot, calendula, caraway, ginger, hyssop, lavender, lemon balm, mint, poppy, rose, rose geranium, rosemary, and violet.

Even with cakes and cookies I sometimes remain in a virtuous mood and use whole wheat flour, preferably a soft-wheat pastry type, available at larger groceries or by mail order, because it yields a finer-textured product.

I also like to use honey steeped with herbs or an herb-flavored sugar in my desserts. These are incredibly easy to make yet deepen the flavor of any dessert. Simply layer herb leaves or flowers with sugar or add to jars of honey. The indispensable flavors are lavender, rose geranium, and lemon balm.

Edible flowers, both sweet and savory, wend their way through all my cooking, but with desserts they take a starring role. Consider the flowers of bergamot, borage, calendula, cinnamon or anise basil, hyssop, lavender, lemon balm, marjoram, nasturtium, rose, rose geranium, rosemary, savory, thyme, and violet. Other edible flowers particularly good with desserts are apple, elderberry, honeysuckle, orange, pinks, plum, rocket, and red clover.

As much as we may care about health and nutrition, there seems to be a basic human need to indulge. Herbs aren't limited to the wholesome desserts. When you're ready to turn to those dessert staples of sugar, butter, eggs, cream, and chocolate, herbs are there to transform them to new heights of decadence.

Note: To substitute dried herbs for fresh, lessen quantities by one-half to two-thirds.

BAKED APPLE SLICES WITH LAVENDER CREAM

Makes 4 servings

Lavender isn't just for linens, as this low-fat version of one of Stephen Lee's best creations shows. Lee is the owner of The Cookbook Cottage in Louisville, Kentucky, and offers a superb selection of new, used, and rare cookbooks as well as cooking classes. Lee really opened my eyes to lavender, not only with this recipe but with ones for a lavender *crème brûlée* and lavender chocolate cupcakes.

4 medium-size cooking apples, such as Granny Smith, Rome Beauty, or Golden Delicious, peeled, cored, cut into thin slices, and sprinkled with 1 teaspoon fresh lemon juice

3 tablespoons unsalted butter or margarine, cut into thin slices

¼ cup firmly packed light brown sugar

¾ cup light ricotta cheese

¼ cup skim milk

1 tablespoon fresh or dried lavender flowers

3 tablespoons honey

Preheat the oven to 375°F and butter four 6-ounce ramekins. Arrange the apple slices in the ramekins. Lay the butter slices evenly over the apples and sprinkle with the brown sugar. Bake for 20 minutes.

While the apples are baking, combine the remaining ingredients in a food processor or blender and process until smooth. After the apples have baked, turn the oven up to 500°F. Pour the creamed mixture over the apples and bake for another 10 minutes. Serve warm.

One of the most versatile dessert herbs, lavender blends well with a large variety of fruits and sweets.

PEARS POACHED IN WHITE WINE WITH HYSSOP

Makes 4 servings

Spicy yet graceful, a well-crafted Gewürztraminer has a clean, crisp flavor, whether made dry or sweet. Coupling it with succulent pears and the minty pungency of hyssop affords an elegant but easily made dessert.

Explore the possibilities of poaching pears with other wines and flavoring the sauce with other liqueurs. Alternatives to hyssop include rosemary, bergamot flowers, angelica, sweet cicely, and lavender flowers.

2 cups Gewürztraminer wine

⅓ cup honey

One 3-inch cinnamon stick

2 whole cloves

Four 3-inch fresh hyssop sprigs

4 lemon slices

4 ripe but firm pears with stems, such as Bartlett, Anjou, or Bosc

3 tablespoons green Chartreuse

3 tablespoons nonfat or low-fat vanilla yogurt

Fresh hyssop flowers

In a medium-size saucepan, combine the wine, honey, cinnamon, cloves, hyssop sprigs, and lemon slices. Bring to a boil over high heat and and cook for 5 minutes. While the poaching liquid is cooking, carefully peel the pears, leaving the stems intact. If necessary, cut a small slice off the bottom so the pears will stand upright. Stand the pears up in the poaching liquid, cover, and reduce the heat to low so the liquid simmers. Cook until the pears can be pierced easily with a toothpick, about 10 minutes. Remove with a slotted spoon and place in individual bowls or goblets.

Remove the cinnamon, cloves, hyssop, and lemon slices and discard. Add the Chartreuse, increase the heat to medium-high, and boil the syrup until reduced by half.

Let cool slightly, then add the yogurt. Pour the sauce around the pears. Serve warm or chilled, garnished with fresh hyssop flowers.

106

PEACH CUSTARD PIE WITH CINNAMON BASIL

Makes one 9-inch pie

For the crust

1½ cups unbleached or whole wheat all-purpose flour

1 teaspoon ground cinnamon

2 teaspoons grated lemon zest

¼ teaspoon salt

½ cup (1 stick) cold unsalted butter or margarine, cut into small pieces

1 large egg yolk

2 tablespoons ice water

For the filling

⅓ cup unsalted butter or margarine at room temperature

⅔ cup honey

1 large egg

½ teaspoon pure vanilla extract

2 tablespoons orange liqueur

2 tablespoons minced fresh cinnamon basil leaves

⅓ cup unbleached or whole wheat all-purpose flour

4 cups (about 2 pounds) peeled, pitted, and sliced fresh peaches

A perfectly ripened peach is a thing of glory. Cinnamon basil provides an exotic, spicy undertone. Savory and hyssop substitute equally well. To make peeling easy, dip peaches in boiling water for 30 seconds, then drain and plunge them into cold water.

To make the crust, mix the flour, cinnamon, zest, and salt in a bowl. Cut in the butter with a pastry blender or 2 knives until the mixture resembles coarse meal. Whisk the egg yolk and ice water together in a small bowl, add it to the flour mixture, and mix with a fork until the mixture is smooth and forms a ball. Wrap the dough in plastic wrap and refrigerate for 1 hour. Roll the dough out on a lightly floured surface until you have a circle 1 1/2 inches larger than a 9-inch pie pan. Then roll the dough a-round the rolling pin and unroll it over the pie pan. Lightly press it evenly into the pan. Trim and crimp the edges.

Preheat the oven to 325°F. To make the filling, cream the butter, then gradually add the honey and beat until light and fluffy. Add the egg, vanilla, liqueur, basil, and flour and beat until thoroughly blended. Arrange the peach slices on the bottom of the pie shell. Pour the batter evenly over the peaches. Bake until the filling is set, about 1 hour. Serve warm or at room temperature.

AKIN' BACK BLUEBERRY-LAVENDER CRUMB CAKE

Makes one 9-inch square

Sybil and Joe Kunkel own a nursery called Akin' Back Farm in La Grange, Kentucky. This treasure from Sybil's kitchen is one of my favorites.

For the cake

4 tablespoons (½ stick) unsalted butter or margarine, at room temperature

½ cup honey

2 large eggs

½ cup milk

2 cups unbleached all-purpose or whole wheat pastry flour

3 teaspoons baking powder

⅛ teaspoon salt

2 cups fresh or thawed frozen blueberries

1 cup blanched sliced almonds

1 tablespoon fresh or dried lavender flowers

1 tablespoon white sesame seeds

For the topping

1 cup firmly packed light brown sugar

2 tablespoons unbleached all-purpose or whole wheat pastry flour

1 stick unsalted butter or margarine at room temperature

1 teaspoon ground cinnamon

1 teaspoon freshly grated nutmeg

Preheat the oven to 375°F. Grease and lightly flour a 9-inch-square baking pan. To make the cake, cream the butter, then gradually add the honey and beat until light and fluffy. Add the eggs and beat well, then mix in the milk. In another bowl, mix together the flour, baking powder, and salt, then add to the creamed mixture and blend well. Fold in the blueberries, almonds, lavender, and sesame seeds. Spread the batter in the prepared pan. Combine the topping ingredients until crumbly, then sprinkle evenly on top of the cake batter. Bake until a toothpick inserted in the center comes out clean, 40 to 45 minutes. Serve the cake warm with ice cream, if desired.

CHOCOLATE- RASPBERRY- MINT CAKE

Makes one 9-inch-square cake

This is an adaptation of a recipe that's been passed around for at least 30 years, and I have no idea of the origin. Despite its unsurpassable simplicity, when served with whipped cream, the best possible chocolate sauce, and fresh raspberries, it looks and tastes quite opulent.

2 cups unbleached all-purpose or whole wheat pastry flour

1 cup sugar

1½ teaspoons baking soda

⅓ cup unsweetened cocoa powder

¼ cup minced fresh spearmint leaves

1 teaspoon pure mint extract

1 tablespoon raspberry vinegar

½ cup (1 stick) unsalted butter or margarine, melted

1¼ cups water

Flavored whipped cream

Chocolate sauce

Fresh raspberries

Fresh mint sprigs

Preheat the oven to 350°F. Sift together the flour, sugar, soda, and cocoa into an ungreased 9-inch square baking pan. Stir in the mint leaves. Make 3 depressions in the flour mixture. Put the mint extract in one, the vinegar in another, and the butter in the third. Add the water to the pan and mix with a fork until the ingredients are blended. Bake until a toothpick inserted in the center comes out clean, about 30 minutes.

Let cool, remove from the pan, and cut into pieces, trimming the crusts, if desired. Serve each piece with whipped cream flavored with white crème de menthe or raspberry liqueur, chocolate sauce, fresh raspberries, and a sprig of fresh mint.

ROSE GERANIUM SAVARIN

Makes one 10-inch Bundt cake

A spectacular cake that makes a stunning dessert for a party, rose geranium savarin relies on the rose-scented leaves to release their essense throughout its moist richness. Bake the batter in muffin pans, with a rose geranium leaf in the bottom of each cup, and you have individual baba cakes. Don't limit your use of rose geranium leaves to this recipe; line the pans of any butter or sponge cake batter with them.

½ cup milk

About 12 rose geranium leaves

2 cups plus 2 tablespoons granulated sugar

¼ teaspoon salt

One ¼-ounce envelope active dry yeast

¼ cup warm water (100° to 115°F)

2 cups unbleached all-purpose flour

4 large eggs, at room temperature

½ cup (1 stick) unsalted butter or margarine, at room temperature

1½ cups water

½ cup rum or orange liqueur

Sweetened whipped cream

Rose geranium flowers

In a small saucepan, combine the milk, 6 of the geranium leaves, 2 tablespoons of the sugar, and the salt. Cook over low heat, stirring occasionally, for 3 minutes. Remove from the heat and let steep for 30 minutes. Remove and discard the geranium leaves.

In a small bowl, combine the yeast and warm water. Let stand for 5 minutes. Cream the butter, then beat in the eggs one at a time. Add the yeast and milk mixtures and the flour. Beat until smooth. Cover and set in a warm place to rise until doubled in size, about 1 to 1 1/2 hours. Stir down.

Butter and flour a 10-inch Bundt pan and line the bottom with about 6 rose geranium leaves, spacing them evenly. Pour the batter into the prepared pan. Cover and let rise until the dough reaches the top, about 45 minutes.

Preheat the oven to 350°F. Bake the cake until firm, golden, and pulling away from the sides of the pan, 45 to 50 minutes.

Meanwhile, make a syrup by boiling the remaining sugar, the water, and the remaining geranium leaves together for 5 minutes. Remove from the heat, then remove and discard the geranium leaves. Stir in the rum.

When the cake is done, turn it out onto a baking sheet with sides. Remove the rose geranium leaves and prick the top of the cake with a fork. Slowly pour the warm syrup over the top and let the cake soak up the syrup until the cake is cool. Transfer the cake to a serving platter, fill the center with sweetened whipped cream, and garnish with rose geranium flowers.

LANICE STEWART'S MINT MERINGUES WITH STRAWBERRIES IN MINT VINEGAR

Makes 4 servings

---

1 quart washed, hulled, and halved fresh strawberries

4 teaspoons mint vinegar

½ cup plus 1 tablespoon sugar

2 large egg whites at room temperature

⅛ teaspoon cream of tartar

1 tablespoon minced fresh mint leaves

Whipped cream (optional)

Fresh mint sprigs

Strawberries steeped with mint vinegar is an adaptation of the Italian custom of using balsamic vinegar with them. Repeating its use in the meringues yields a pretty pastel nest, and the vinegar acts to ensure their successful baking. Nothing compares to homegrown berries, and I rely on the day-neutral ever-bearing 'Tristar' for sweet, firm strawberries all summer long.

Refashion the pairing of fruit and meringue using whole raspberries with raspberry vinegar and bergamot flowers instead of mint, or sliced peaches with cinnamon basil vinegar and calendula flowers.

Place the strawberries in a glass bowl. Sprinkle 1 tablespoon of the vinegar and 1 tablespoon of the sugar over the berries; stir gently . Cover and refrigerate for up to 4 hours.

Using a grease-free stainless-steel or copper bowl, beat the egg whites until foamy and opaque with an electric mixer at high speed. Add the cream of tartar and beat until soft peaks form. Continuing to beat at high speed, add the remaining sugar 1 tablespoon at a time, beating well after each addition. Add the remaining vinegar and the mint. Beat until the meringue appears shiny and stiff peaks form.

Cover a baking sheet with parchment paper. Using a pastry bag with a 1/2-inch round or star-shaped tip, make a 3-inch circle of meringue on the parchment. Fill in evenly with meringue to form the base. Pipe two more layers on top around the edge. Alternatively, put a large spoonful of the meringue on the parchment to make a nest about 3 inches in diameter. Using a smaller spoon, shape the nest with a depressed center, being sure not to make the bottom or sides too thin. Make 3 additional nests, spacing them about 2 inches apart. Set the meringues in a cold oven, then turn the heat to 250°F. Bake for 1 hour. Turn the oven off and leave the meringues in the oven for another hour. Remove the meringues and allow to cool. Use a spatula to remove them from the parchment. If desired, store meringues for several days in an airtight container.

To serve, divide the berries among the meringue shells. Garnish with whipped cream, if desired, and fresh sprigs of mint.

WHITE CHOCOLATE-VIOLET MOUSSE

Makes 4 servings

In *The Essence of Paradise*, a book on fragrant plants, Tovah Martin writes, "Violets possess an essence so provocative that it's impossible to inhale the perfume once and then walk away." The ethereal quality of violets is echoed in this whipped cloud of a dessert. The most intoxicatingly scented are the tender, double-flowering hybrids of *Viola odorata* known as Parma violets. The single-flowering species and its dusky rose variant, *Viola odorata rosea*, will do admirably in this softly shaded flummery. Use only the finest white chocolate that is all cocoa butter.

Candied violets are easily made, as described below. They can also be bought at gourmet food stores.

½ cup fresh violet flowers
¼ cup boiling water
½ pound white chocolate, grated
¼ cup sugar
2 large egg whites, at room temperature
1 cup heavy whipping cream
fresh or candied violets

Remove and discard the green portion behind the violet petals. Put the petals in a small bowl and pour the boiling water over them. Cover and let infuse overnight. Strain and reserve.

Place the chocolate in the top of a double boiler over simmering water. Stir as the chocolate melts. Remove from heat and set aside.

Combine the violet water with the sugar in a small saucepan. Stirring frequently, cook over medium heat until a candy thermometer registers 240°F, soft ball stage. Remove from heat.

Beat the egg whites with an electric mixer at medium speed in a grease-free stainless-steel or copper mixing bowl until soft peaks form. Continuing to beat at medium speed, slowly pour the hot syrup in a thin stream into the egg whites. Continuing to beat, slowly add the melted chocolate. Turn the mixer speed to high and beat for 3 minutes.

In another bowl, beat the whipping cream with clean mixers until stiff peaks form, then fold gently into the chocolate mixture. Spoon the mousse into parfait glasses or sorbet goblets and chill for at least 4 hours. Garnish with fresh or candied violets.

To candy violet flowers, beat an egg white until frothy, then coat all flower surfaces with it using a camel's hair brush. Sprinkle with superfine sugar, colored to match the flower if desired. Place on wax paper to dry for 2 days. Store in a tightly closed container for up to a year. Candy other flowers like borage, rose petals, rosemary, and rose geranium, as well as small mint or rose geranium leaves.

WINE SORBET WITH HERBS

Makes 1 quart

Whether served in crystal goblets with silver spoons as a palate refresher between courses of a formal dinner or eaten out of a plastic bowl on the back-door step, the fragrance and flavor of homemade herbal sorbets makes them a pleasant interlude.

This is another recipe that invites you to experiment to your heart's content. Play with different wines and herb combinations. The first herbs that come to mind are rose petals, lavender flowers, bergamot flowers, scented geranium leaves, mint, angelica, sweet cicely, lemon balm, lemon verbena, anise and cinnamon basils, and anise hyssop. But how intriguing to make a sorbet that mirrors May wine, using sweet woodruff and a Riesling, then serving it with a strawberry sauce. Using nasturtium or Mexican marigold mint would definitely keep people awake between courses.

Rosé and blush wines lend a lovely tint to sorbet. Look, too, for wines with a pineapple or berry flavor. Light red wines go well with the savory herbs like rosemary, thyme, and sage.

The easiest ice cream maker to use is the kind in which the inner container is pre-chilled.

1 cup sugar

2 cups wine

2 cups water

½ cup fresh or ¼ cup dried herbs

⅓ cup fresh lemon juice

In a medium-size saucepan, combine the sugar, wine, and water and bring to a boil over high heat, stirring occasionally. Reduce the heat to low and simmer for 5 minutes. Remove from the heat, stir in the herbs, and cool to room temperature. Strain, then stir in the lemon juice. Chill in the refrigerator for 1 to 2 hours.

Freeze the mixture in an ice cream maker according to the manufacturer's directions. Or pour it into ice cube trays or a large flat baking pan; when the mixture is mushy, remove it from the freezer and stir with a fork, pour into a bowl, and beat with a mixer or blend in a food processor until smooth. Freeze again until firm or repeat several more times.

MAGGIE HOUPT'S BUTTERMILK HERB COOKIES

Makes about 36 cookies, depending on size

My mother fondly recalls how eagerly she looked forward to these cookies being packed in her lunch box. They were made with freshly churned butter and real buttermilk, from the family's Guernsey and Jersey cows, and an egg from the barnyard chickens. My grandmother rolled them thick and shaped the cookies with a tin cookie cutter made by Grandad, which I still have. Icing was only for special occasions, however.

Use your favorite sweet herbs or flowers plus any other herbs you like for flavoring these uncomplicated cookies. Some of the best herb seeds for these cookies are those of angelica, anise, coriander, fennel, poppy, and sweet cicely.

½ cup (1 stick) unsalted butter or margarine, at room temperature

1 cup granulated sugar

1 large egg

1 teaspoon pure vanilla extract

1 tablespoon minced fresh herbs or 2 teaspoons crushed herb seeds

½ cup buttermilk, plus extra for the glaze

½ teaspoon baking soda

2 cups unbleached all-purpose or whole wheat pastry flour

1 teaspoon baking powder

¼ teaspoon salt

½ cup confectioners' sugar

Preheat the oven to 350°F. In a large bowl, cream the butter, then add the sugar, beating until light and fluffy. Add the egg, vanilla, and herbs and beat thoroughly. Stir the baking soda into the buttermilk. In another bowl, mix the flour, baking powder, and salt together. In 3 batches, alternately add the buttermilk and flour mixtures to the creamed mixture, blending well after each addition. Cover and chill for 30 minutes.

Roll out the dough on a lightly floured board to about 1/8 to 1/4 inch thick, cut into shapes with cookie cutters, and put on greased or parchment-covered baking sheets or one coated with a nonstick cooking spray. Bake until lightly browned, 8 to 10 minutes. Remove and cool on wire racks.

Combine the confectioners' sugar with enough buttermilk to make an icing; spread on the cooled cookies. Store in an airtight container.

ROSE GERANIUM-MADEIRA COOKIES

Makes 2 dozen cookies

These quaint, sentimentally inspired cookies, combining as they do two relics of the Victorian era, are ideally suited for serving as dessert with the Wine Sorbet with Herbs (page 114) or for lunch with fresh fruit.

Rose water is available at health food or gourmet food stores or from mail-order sources.

1 large egg

⅔ cup plus 3 tablespoons sugar

3 tablespoons unsalted butter or margarine, at room temperature

2 cups unbleached all-purpose or whole wheat pastry flour

2 teaspoons baking powder

½ teaspoon salt

2 tablespoons minced fresh rose geranium leaves

⅓ cup sweet or medium-sweet Madeira

2 teaspoons rose water

1 teaspoon ground cardamom seeds

24 small rose geranium leaves or flowers

Preheat the oven to 350°F. Beat the egg until lemon colored, then add 2/3 cup sugar and butter and beat until light and fluffy. In another bowl, combine the flour, baking powder, salt, and minced rose geranium leaves, then add to the egg mixture alternately with the Madeira. Add the rose water, mix well, and chill 30 minutes. Combine the 3 tablespoons of sugar and cardamom in a small dish. Roll the dough into 1-inch balls, then roll in the sugar-cardamom mixture. Place the balls on a greased or parchment-covered baking sheet or one coated with a nonstick cooking spray. Leave 2 inches between cookies. Press a rose geranium leaf or flower well into the cookie. Bake until lightly browned, 8 to 10 minutes. Remove and cool on wire racks. Store in an airtight container.

ROSE PETAL MADELEINES

Makes 24 madeleines

Ephemeral madeleines, fragrant with rose petals in the buttery center beneath the crisp shell-shaped crust, capture the romantic spirit of genteel days long gone.

Rose water is available at health food and gourmet food stores and from mail-order sources.

¾ cup (1½ sticks) unsalted butter

3 large eggs, at room temperature

⅔ cup granulated sugar

1 cup unbleached all-purpose or pastry flour

1 tablespoon rose water

½ cup minced fresh rose petals

Confectioners' sugar

Clarify the butter by melting it in a heatproof glass measuring cup set in a pot of hot water, then bringing the water to a boil and cooking until the clear liquid separates from the milky whey of the butter at the bottom. Pour off the clear liquid and let sit until cool but still liquid. Preheat the oven to 375°F and butter the madeleine molds.

In a mixing bowl, beat the eggs and sugar together until the mixture is pale yellow, thick, and forms a ribbon when the beater is lifted. Sift the flour into the egg mixture in 3 batches, folding it in gently after each addition. Add the butter, rose water, and rose petals, folding in thoroughly but gently.

Spoon the batter into the prepared madeleine pan, filling the molds three-quarters full. Bake until light golden brown, about 10 minutes. Turn out onto a wire rack and sift confectioners' sugar lightly onto the shell side. Serve within hours, if not minutes.

LEMON-CALENDULA BARS

Makes 2 to 3 dozen bars

In the sixteenth century calendula was considered to have enough magical power to assist in seeing not only fairies but also one's future husband. No promises are made for this version of a classic cookie, but it can be considered seductive.

Orange-flower water is available at health food and gourmet food stores and ethnic markets.

> *1 cup (2 sticks) unsalted butter or margarine, at room temperature*
>
> *¾ cup confectioners' sugar*
>
> *Grated zest of 1 lemon*
>
> *1 tablespoon orange-flower water or orange liqueur*
>
> *1½ cups unbleached all-purpose or whole wheat pastry flour*
>
> *5 large eggs*
>
> *2 cups granulated sugar*
>
> *6 tablespoons fresh lemon juice*
>
> *½ cup minced fresh calendula petals*

Preheat the oven to 350°F. Grease a 9- by 13-inch pan or coat with a nonstick cooking spray. In a large bowl, cream the butter, then gradually add 1/2 cup of the confectioners' sugar, the zest, and orange-flower water and beat until light and fluffy. Gradually add 1-1/4 cups of the flour, mixing until combined well. Spread evenly in the pan. Bake until lightly browned, 15 or 20 minutes.

Meanwhile, combine the eggs, granulated sugar, lemon juice, calendula petals, and the remaining flour. Pour the mixture over the crust and return it to the oven until the filling is set, another 20 minutes. Sift the remaining confectioners' sugar over the warm cookies. Let cool, then cut into bars and remove from the pan. Store in an airtight container.

Sauces, Dressings, Preserves, Condiments, and Beverages

Herb vinegars, mustard, salsa, jelly, and oil

Many of the common herbs are available fresh at markets year-round, and some herbs grow readily indoors during the winter or in a coldframe outdoors, the best of which is the double-walled type. Even with these options, using preserved herbs is a time-honored alternative. Flavoring vinegars, oils, mustards, butters, seasoning blends, jellies, and jams with herbs yields something greater than the sum of the parts.

Still, having the herbs, plain and simple, may be what you want instead. For this we can turn to the age-old methods of drying or salting herbs, plus freezing. For preserving you'll want the most intense flavor, when the essential oils are greatest. Usually this is just as the flowers begin to open. For seeds, gather when they turn from green to brown but before they fall. Dig roots in the autumn. Gather herbs in the morning after the dew has dried but before the sun is high and hot. Cut plants back about halfway. Wash, if necessary, and shake off excess water.

To dry herbs at room temperature, tie several stems together and hang them upside down in a dark, dry, warm, well-ventilated place. Or spread herbs out flat on screens. To oven-dry, use an oven with a pilot light or set at its lowest setting, with herbs spread out on a cheesecloth-lined tray. Drying time by any of these methods depends on the conditions.

When herbs feel totally dry, remove the leaves from the stems. Loosely pack in small jars and cap tightly. Store in a dark, cool, dry place. Check for condensation after a week and dry in a warm place if necessary. Dried homegrown herbs keep their flavor for about a year.

Place seed heads upside down in a paper bag and let dry in a dark area until the seeds fall out. Store tightly covered.

Basil, fennel, dill, parsley, chervil, chives, and burnet are better frozen. Remove the leaves from the stems and store in small plastic freezer bags.

Salting is used with basil and tarragon. Alternate thin layers of kosher salt and leaves in a covered jar or crock.

Note: To substitute dried herbs for fresh, lessen quantities by one-half to two-thirds.

Herb Vinegars

Although making herb-flavored vinegars is often one of the first ways people want to use their homegrown herbs, once made, they frequently become more kitchen decoration than culinary essential. Certainly salads, pickles, and marinades are the most obvious object of vinegar's piquant favor, but that is only the beginning.

Let vinegar substitute for lemon or lime juices with both raw and cooked vegetables as well as with fish, poultry, and other meats. Vinegar can also replace all or part of the wine called for in a recipe and is especially good for deglazing a pan. Stews, soups, and sauces get a bright pop of flavor when vinegar is added near the end of cooking. Even beverages, fruits, and desserts can benefit from the addition of vinegars.

Because herb vinegars are meant to embellish and emphasize, they need to be strong and made not only with the best ingredients but also with techniques that won't corrupt their veracity.

Adding a sprig or two of an herb to a bottle of vinegar may give off a hauntingly delicate scent, but the effect in food will be negligible. The bottom line is this: use lots of herbs and other flavorings. A cup of loosely packed fresh, clean, dry leaves or flowers to a pint of vinegar is not too much. Depending on the flavors you want, other additions might include a tablespoon each of crushed herb seeds or whole spices, several garlic cloves or slices of fresh ginger or horseradish, fresh or dried hot pepper, strips of citrus peel, bay leaves, or edible flowers.

As to the quality of the ingredients, most obviously important is the vinegar itself. Although sometimes I make my own, generally I buy the vinegar. Distilled white vinegar is an excellent window cleaner, but it is harsh-tasting, quickly produced, and unsuitable for flavoring. Many apple cider vinegars are merely distilled white vinegar with caramel coloring and a little flavoring. Be sure to read the label's fine print. Instead I choose to prowl the aisles of gourmet, Asian, and health food stores

for high-quality vinegars made from the likes of fruit, red or white wines, sherry, champagne, or rice wine. Don't panic if the vinegar has a sediment in the bottom, because this is vinegar "mother," a by-product of the organism responsible for its existence, and it proves you've got a natural product.

As to the methodology for making herb-flavored vinegars, the biggest misconception is that the vinegar should be heated. Heating impairs the composition of the vinegar and volatilizes the herb's essential oils. Only if you are adding whole spices or seeds should the vinegar be warmed to about 110°F. Allow it to cool before adding fresh herbs or other ingredients.

Never use aluminum kitchen utensils, because the vinegar will react to them; instead use glass, stainless steel, plastic, or enamel.

Neither should herb vinegars be steeped or stored in bright light. Always keep them in a cool, dark place.

Although stores offer lovely glass bottles that can be used for herb vinegars, I prefer to recycle bottles ranging in size from 8 to 16 ounces. Metal lids corrode, so corks must be used as stoppers. Hardware stores carry generic corks, while wine-making shops also have the plastic-topped cork caps.

Herb vinegars make lovely gifts. To seal and decorate the bottles, I drape a ribbon across the top and dip the top of the bottle several times in melted paraffin. The end of the ribbon extends below the wax so it can be lifted to remove the wax and open the bottle. Finally, I add a hand-decorated label and a circlet of dried herbs around the neck of the bottle.

Vinegars made with the quantities of herbs suggested here will be usable within a day or two. In fact, you can even refill the bottle after each use for the equivalent of several bottles until all the flavor is extracted. Make sure the herbs are always either completely immersed or removed as the vinegar is used. If desired, strain flavored vinegars through a double thickness of cheesecloth or a paper coffee filter and then rebottle them, adding a few fresh herb sprigs.

Some suggested combinations for herb vinegars:
- White wine vinegar, lavender flowers, and orange peel
- Red wine vinegar, garlic cloves, bay, rosemary, thyme, oregano, marjoram, parsley, lemon peel, and fennel
- Red wine vinegar, basil, oregano, garlic cloves, and dried hot pepper
- Rice wine vinegar, garlic cloves, dried hot pepper, fresh ginger, lemongrass, coriander leaves (cilantro), spearmint, cinnamon and/or Thai basil, and star anise
- White wine or champagne vinegar, clove pink flowers, and whole cloves
- White or rice wine or champagne vinegar, dill leaves, flowers, and seeds, lemon peel, and garlic chives
- White or rice wine or champagne vinegar, rose petals, and rose geranium leaves
- Pure cider vinegar, garlic cloves, shallots, bay, thyme, sage, parsley, marjoram, caraway, and lovage
- White or rice wine or champagne vinegar, anise leaves and seeds, anise hyssop flowers, fennel seeds and leaves, chervil, and tarragon
- Champagne vinegar, mint, and violet flowers
- White or rice wine or champagne vinegar, sweet woodruff, marjoram, fresh ginger, and black peppercorns
- Red wine or cider vinegar, garlic cloves, shallots, bay, thyme, dried hot pepper, sage, parsley, horseradish root, allspice berries, whole cloves, juniper berries, black peppercorns, and coriander seeds
- White or rice wine or champagne vinegar, lemon balm, lemon verbena, lemon thyme, lemon basil, lemongrass, and lemon peel
- White or rice wine or champagne vinegar and any edible flowers, including calendula, nasturtiums, mint, basil, scented geraniums, Mexican marigold mint, pineapple sage, or bergamot
- White or rice wine or champagne vinegar, parsley, mint, garlic cloves, whole cloves, black peppercorns, and freshly grated nutmeg
- White or rice wine or champagne vinegar, burnet, borage leaves and flowers, and garlic chives
- Pure cider vinegar, sage, shallots, rosemary, bay, and nasturtium flowers
- Sherry vinegar, fresh ginger, garlic chives, and a cinnamon stick
- Champagne vinegar, orange peel, and orange mint
- Sherry vinegar, hyssop, lemon balm, lemon thyme, and black peppercorns

Herb Oils

With such chefs as Jean-Georges Vongerichten pioneering the way from the New York Restaurant Lafayette and Jo Jo, herb oils are destined to be the new stars from the kitchen herb garden. As we learn to make do with less and less butter, herb-infused oils offer an alternative that sacrifices nothing in terms of flavor.

Drizzle them on *bruschetta*, mix them in marinades, make inspired vinaigrettes, sprinkle them over cooked vegetables, and, of course, use them anytime for sautéing.

Herb oils fall into three categories: those made from fresh leaves, fresh roots, or ground seeds. Each is made in a slightly different way.

The best oils to use are expeller-processed and unrefined, and I often buy organic ones. Expeller processing produces oil without the use of chemical solvents. My preferences for most purposes are extra virgin or virgin olive oils and light sesame oil available form health food stores. Canola, safflower, sunflower, avocado, almond, walnut, and hazelnut oils are all "healthy" oils in terms of their physiological benefits and minimum of pollutants, compared to other oils.

To make an herb oil from any leafy herb, whether by itself or in combination, use 1/2 cup minced herbs to 1 cup of oil. Combine in a clean jar and shake well. Let stand at room temperature for several days. Carefully decant the oil from the herbs or strain through a double thickness of cheesecloth or a paper coffee filter, cap tightly, and label. Both olive and sesame oils are relatively stable at room temperature, so these can be kept in a cabinet, away from heat. All other oils should be refrigerated after opening.

To prepare root herbs like garlic, horseradish, shallots, or ginger, peel and finely mince 2 tablespoons for each 2 cups of oil. Combine in a clean glass jar and let sit at room temperature for 2 hours, then strain, label, cover tightly, and store.

Seeds like anise, caraway, coriander, cumin, dill, fennel, and mustard, plus dry herbs or spices like saffron or paprika, are best ground and mixed with a small amount of water—3 tablespoons ground herb to 1 tablespoon water—to make a thick paste. Place in a clean jar and cover with 2 cups of oil. Tightly cap the jar and shake. Allow to steep at room temperature for 2 days, shaking occasionally. Let the herbs settle, then filter the oil, bottle, cap tightly, label, and store.

To create herb oils from a mixture of herb leaves, seeds, and roots plus spices, mince the leaves, peel the roots and cut into small pieces, and lightly crush the seeds. Steep for several days, then strain, cover tightly, label, and store.

Do not leave any herbs in the oils for decoration since there is the potential for food poisoning.

Some suggested combinations for herb oils:
- Dill leaves and seeds, garlic, and burnet
- Coriander leaves (cilantro), oregano, dried hot pepper, and garlic
- Rosemary, thyme, marjoram, fennel leaves, and garlic
- Tarragon, green peppercorns, and lemon balm
- Coriander leaves (cilantro), mint, garlic, and dried hot pepper
- Coriander leaves (cilantro), Thai basil, lemongrass, fresh ginger, and garlic
- Basil, garlic, lemon thyme, burnet, and chives
- Horseradish, shallots, thyme, and mustard seeds
- Anise, fennel, and tarragon
- Basil, garlic chives, marjoram, and oregano
- Lemon basil, lemon thyme, and rosemary
- Shallots, thyme, and rosemary

Herb Vinaigrettes and Salad Dressings

Long gone are the days when most Americans thought a salad consisted of a pallid wedge of iceberg lettuce topped with a viscous orange fluid euphemistically referred to as French dressing. Now, produce departments, farmer's markets, and especially seed catalogs, most notable being *The Cook's Garden*, offer an extensive range of exotica from chard to claytonia, curly mallow, dandelion, curly endive, good King Henry, mâche, mizuna, purple mustard, plantain, purslane, red orache, and shungiku. Plus, the dozens of looseleaf, butterhead, crisphead, and romaine lettuce varieties for spring, summer, fall, or winter growing are enough to make a salad spinner dizzy.

The tie that binds this cosmopolitan world together is the dressing. With a pantry filled with herb-flavored vinegars, oils, and mustards, you can quickly and easily prepare unique, tailor-made vinaigrettes. All that's needed is a small bowl and a whisk or a jar with a lid.

BASIC HERB VINAIGRETTE

Makes about 3/4 cup

Vinaigrette recipes used to call for three or four times as much oil as vinegar, but I use less. Good-quality vinegar has a mellowness that is not overpowering and so can be used in greater proportion. For low-fat versions, substitute broth or stock, fresh tomato puree, fresh carrot juice, or buttermilk for the oil. Adding yogurt, tofu, or cheese is especially recommended when the salad contains some of the stronger or more bitter greens and herbs, since these tend to mellow the flavors.

Shoyu is a Japanese soy sauce that is lower in salt; it is available at health food stores.

½ cup extra virgin olive or other oil

¼ cup red or white wine or other vinegar

1 to 2 teaspoons fresh lemon juice

½ teaspoon honey (optional)

1 to 2 teaspoons Dijon or other prepared mustard

½ teaspoon salt or shoyu

1 to 4 tablespoons minced fresh herb leaves or crushed seeds

¼ to ½ teaspoon freshly ground black pepper

1 garlic clove, minced (optional)

1 to 4 tablespoons nonfat or low-fat plain yogurt, soft tofu, or crumbled cheese, such as blue, Parmesan, or feta (optional)

Combine all the ingredients in a small bowl and whisk or place in a lidded jar and shake for 10 seconds. Use immediately or refrigerate for up to 3 weeks, shaking well before serving.

SESAME-HERB DRESSING

Makes 1½ cups

This is not your run-of-the-mill dressing. The ingredients may be unfamiliar, but the creamy taste and delicate color should mollify even the staid. Tahini, made from ground hulled sesame seeds, is a high-protein, nutrient-rich food with a nutty flavor. It is most readily found in health food stores.

½ cup tahini

½ cup nonfat or low-fat plain yogurt

½ cup grated raw carrot

2 tablespoons fresh lemon juice

2 tablespoons balsamic vinegar

2 tablespoons minced fresh parsley leaves

1 tablespoon minced fresh spearmint leaves

1 tablespoon minced fresh coriander (cilantro) leaves

½ teaspoon hot red pepper sauce

Using a food processor or blender, combine all the ingredients until smooth. Keep refrigerated up to a week.

Salsas

Like firecrackers, a succession of flavors explodes from a well-made salsa. Most Americans first came to encounter salsa, Spanish for "sauce," with the widespread advent of southwestern and Mexican cooking, but other cuisines have similar condiments. Whether they answer to salsa, sambal, chutney, or relish, their raison d'être is that they are quickly and easily made, require little or no cooking, utilize any number of ingredients, can be varied in any number of ways, and contain almost no fat. These intensely flavored and scented compositions of fresh vegetables, fruits, herbs, hot peppers, vinegar, and spices improve whatever they may accompany.

FRESH TOMATO SALSA

Makes 2 cups

If, as John Steinbeck wrote, beans put a roof on your stomach, does the omnipresent southwestern tomato salsa become the fire or the windows?

1 pound ripe tomatoes, peeled and seeded (see page 31), then finely chopped (about 2 cups)

½ cup thinly sliced scallions, both white and green parts

1 to 2 serrano, jalapeño, or poblano peppers, fresh or roasted and peeled (see note), cored, seeded, and chopped

1 garlic clove, minced

1 to 2 tablespoons minced fresh parsley leaves (to taste)

1 to 2 tablespoons minced fresh coriander (cilantro) leaves (to taste)

1 teaspoon minced fresh oregano leaves

1 tablespoon red wine vinegar or fresh lime juice

1 tablespoon extra virgin olive oil

Salt and freshly ground black pepper to taste

Combine all the ingredients in a nonreactive bowl, cover, and allow the flavors to blend for several hours before serving, pouring off any excess liquid if desired. This will keep for about a week.

Note: Hot peppers can be roasted and peeled like bell peppers (see page 71). When handling, wear rubber gloves or wash hands very thoroughly with hot, soapy water.

TOMATILLO SALSA (SALSA VERDE)

Makes about 2 cups

Sometimes called *green tomatoes*, native Mexican tomatillos belong to the same family but are more closely related to the Chinese lantern plant and cape gooseberry. Borne on sprawling plants that are easily grown and quite prolific, the round fruit wrapped in a papery husk has a lemony flavor. A rare purple variety from Seeds Blüm, Nichols Garden Nursery, and Seeds of Change makes an unusually colored salsa. Carry through the color scheme with purple bell peppers.

1 pound fresh tomatillos

1 to 2 serrano, jalapeño, or poblano peppers, fresh or roasted with the tomatillos and peeled, cored, seeded, and chopped (to taste)

1 small garlic clove, minced

4 scallions, both white and green parts, thinly sliced

1 tablespoon fresh lime juice

½ to 1 cup loosely packed minced fresh coriander (cilantro) leaves (to taste)

2 tablespoons minced fresh lemon thyme leaves (optional)

Remove the husks from the tomatillos, rinse, and prepare by either boiling or roasting. To boil, bring 1/2 cup water to a boil over medium-high heat, add the tomatillos, reduce the heat to low, and simmer, covered, until softened, about 5 minutes. To roast, place the tomatillos on a baking sheet in a preheated 400°F oven until skins blister, about 20 minutes.

Using a food processor or blender, combine all the ingredients and puree until coarsely chopped.

The salsa can be stored tightly covered in the refrigerator for 3 to 5 days.

ROSE MARIE NICHOLS MCGEE'S THAI SALSA

Makes about 2 cups

This is adapted from Nichols Garden Nursery in Albany, Oregon, a company specializing in unusual herb and vegetable seeds plus an interesting assortment of garden and kitchen items.

2 medium-size cucumbers, peeled, seeded, and coarsely chopped (1½ pounds)

1 teaspoon salt

¼ cup minced Thai or other fresh basil leaves

3 tablespoons coarsely chopped peanuts

3 tablespoons minced yellow onion

1 fresh jalapeño pepper, stems removed, seeded, and chopped

2 tablespoons white wine vinegar

2 tablespoons honey

2 tablespoons sesame oil

Combine the cucumber and salt and let sit for 30 minutes, then drain. Combine with the remaining ingredients, then chill until ready to serve. The salsa can be stored tightly covered in the refrigerator for 3 to 5 days.

MINT CHUTNEY

Makes about 1 cup

Because there are so many different scents and flavors of mint, they invite experimentation. Besides spearmint and peppermint, ginger and lemon mints would be logical to try with this fresh sauce. If using apple, orange, or pineapple mint, include the appropriate diced fresh fruit and juice. The yogurt cools the chutney down, but it can be left out if desired.

Other options include making this with all fresh coriander (cilantro) or all fresh parsley or a combination thereof, perhaps with a small amount of mint or thyme.

2 cups loosely packed minced fresh mint leaves

1 cup loosely packed minced fresh parsley leaves

½ cup thinly sliced scallions, both white and green parts

1 tablespoon minced fresh ginger

2 garlic cloves, minced

½ teaspoon ground cayenne pepper or hot red pepper sauce

1 tablespoon fresh lemon or lime juice

1 teaspoon grated lemon or lime zest

¼ to ½ cup nonfat or low-fat plain yogurt

1 tablespoon mint vinegar

Combine all the ingredients in a serving bowl. You can also prepare this chutney in a food processor, pulsing several times so as not to overprocess. Cover and allow the flavors to blend for several hours before serving. Keeps for 1 to 2 days in the refrigerator.

Rose Marie Nichols McGee's Thai Salsa
Tomatillo Salsa
Fresh Tomato Salsa

PESTO

In less than half a century, pesto has risen from obscurity in American cookbooks and kitchens to its present phoenix state. What hermit among us does not know that pesto is a sauce of Italian origin made from fresh basil, garlic, cheese, olive oil, and pine nuts? Or that the word itself means "pounded," taken from the age-old method of grinding said ingredients together in a mortar and pestle? Who, too, has not brought an expensive little tub of the green paste home from the grocery and subsequently wondered what all the fuss was about?

Yes, there are small producers of pesto who carefully and lovingly produce a choice sauce for purchase, but time does not treat our hero well. I'm not even particularly fond of my own homemade pesto that's been frozen or chilled very long. To my mind and tongue, pesto should really be savored only from just-picked basil, made promptly, and eaten in a timely fashion.

Given that basil is a most easily grown and vigorous plant, even in containers, and that many mail-order herb and seed sources offer at least ten different varieties of the "king of herbs," the bottom line is that there is no excuse for not making your own pesto.

How, then, to begin? There are as many recipes as there are cooks. John Thorne, author of *Simple Cooking*, in an erudite essay on the subject, writes, "In pesto, as in many other recipes, there are variables beyond the control of the writer—basil has different intensities, cheeses (even of the same name) are bolder or tamer, and even your own palate changes from day to day…it is better to work…from a sense of where you want to end up."

In other words, if on some days you want more cheese, then by all means add it. Perhaps parsley, lemon, butter, cream, ricotta, or pancetta may attract on another day. Full-flavored and aromatic Genoese basil sends out the siren's call one morning, while the sweet, mellow leaves of Napoletano basil beckon on another. Some heretics even use other herbs, usually combining three parts basil or parsley with one part coriander (cilantro), garlic chives, fennel, mint, oregano, rosemary, sage, savory, sorrel, spinach, tarragon, thyme, or watercress. Walnuts are the most common substitute for pine nuts, but certainly others have been tried. Sardo pecorino, a sharply flavored sheep's milk cheese, is the most authentic cheese, but blander, more readily available Parmesan and Romano cheeses have become accepted.

Making pesto in a mortar and pestle is as good or better than Nautilus equipment as upper-body work, so, thankfully, a food processor with the plastic blade makes a pesto with authentic texture, given the garlic is crushed first. The metal blade produces a finer-textured pesto. Most important is not to overprocess.

For initial proportions, try 2 cups loosely packed fresh basil leaves, a large pinch of salt, and 1 or 2 garlic cloves. Process into a paste that still retains its bright green color. (If using a blender, the basil, salt, and garlic must be processed with the oil.)

Next, incorporate some combination of freshly grated Sardo pecorino, Parmesan, and/or Romano cheese, never using more than 1/2 cup for 2 cups basil. With the processor running, add extra virgin olive oil, first drop by drop, then slowly in a thin stream, until you have the consistency you want, or about 1/2 cup. Finally, process in 1/4 to 1/2 cup pine nuts. If desired, add a tablespoon of butter or cream now as well.

The verdant ambrosia thus prepared, it is ready to be tossed with hot pasta or gnocchi. Depending on preference, 1/2 to 1 cup of pesto is needed for 1 pound of pasta. Other traditional uses include serving it as a sauce for grilled or poached fish or chicken, as a dressing for tomato slices, or stirring it into minestrone soup. Entire books have been written on other uses, some more appetizing than others but all worthy of consideration nonetheless. Most notable are pesto with potato or bulgur salads, with smoked mussels over pasta, in omelets, and on pizza.

Pesto not used immediately can be stored for weeks, some say months, in the refrigerator with a 1/2-inch coating of olive oil on top. Some people are also content to freeze pesto—without the cheese—in small containers, adding 1/2 inch olive oil to the top; add the cheese after thawing and use within 6 months.

FRESH TOMATO-BASIL SAUCE

Makes 4 to 6 servings

The two stars in the firmament of the summer food garden are basil and tomatoes, and no two foods are so closely associated.

Considered a holy herb in its native India, basil has a surprisingly intense scent of clove and pepper with hints of sweetness and licorice as well. Different species and strains from around the world give us basils of varying statures, leaf sizes and colors, scents, and flavors. The basils grown for cooking can be divided into five types: sweet, bush, lettuce-leaf, purple, and scented.

Sweet basil (*Ocimum basilicum*) has long, smooth, glossy leaves. The best-flavored basil is variously labeled 'Sweet Genovese', 'Genova Profumatissima', or 'Perfume Basil'.

Bush basil (*O. basilicum* var. *minimum*) forms a mound 12 inches tall with tiny 1-inch leaves, making it especially ornamental and particularly good for container growing. Among the varieties available, 'Fino Verde', or 'Fine Green', is considered the most desirable. Although not strong in flavor, the 6-inch 'Spicy Globe' can be grown indoors easily, along with the more pungent 'Greek Mini' form.

Lettuce-leaf basils (*O. basilicum* var. *crispum*) have exceptionally large leaves, often up to 4 inches long and wide, that are wavy or crinkly. This attribute has been selected for in the ornamental 'Green Ruffles'. Mildly spicy, 'Mammoth' and 'Napoletano' are good for including fresh in salads, using as food wrappers, or adding to slow- cooked sauces.

The countenance of purple-leaf basil (*O. basilicum* var. *purpurascens*) fits its common name. With crinkled leaves and robust mien, 'Purple Ruffles' is the choice for beauty, but the less vigorous 'Dark Opal' is preferred for use fresh in salads or to impart color and flavor to vinegars and jellies. Cinnamon and anise basils (both variants of *O. basilicum*) and lemon basil (*O. americanum*, formerly *O. citriodorum*) bear the essence of their namesakes. The anise and lemon are the basils of choice for Asian cooking, but they work in any other way that basils do. All three are lovely in desserts as well. Plus, lemon basil is ignored by Japanese beetles!

The ephemeral essential oils of basil are always best preserved when added near the end of cooking, so to bring the finest of any of these basil varieties together with the most flavorful of sun-ripened tomatoes in a dish that needs no cooking on a sultry summer day seems almost too good to be true. There are no hard-and-fast rules for this rustic sauce. Follow the dictates of mood and appetite.

Certainly gardeners have strong opinions as to what constitutes a good tomato, but from among the dozens of heirloom and modern varieties, I suggest the French 'Dona' or 'Marmande', the Italian heirloom 'Costoluto Genovese', the American heirlooms 'Brandywine' and 'German Red', and the high-vitamin-A 'Caro Rich'.

1½ pounds ripe tomatoes, peeled and seeded (see page 31), then chopped (about 3 cups)

12 to 24 medium-size fresh basil leaves, torn into pieces (to taste)

2 to 4 tablespoons minced fresh herb leaves, such as chives, garlic chives, Italian (flat-leaf) parsley, tarragon, or thyme (to taste)

½ pound fresh mozzarella cheese, diced (optional)

½ cup extra virgin olive oil

Salt and freshly ground black pepper to taste

1 pound dry pasta, cooked al dente according to package instructions, and drained

Freshly grated Parmesan cheese (optional)

In a bowl, combine the tomatoes, basil, other herbs, mozzarella, oil, salt, and pepper, mixing well. Let stand at room temperature for 1 hour. Toss the cooked pasta with the sauce, adding grated Parmesan if desired.

Horseradish Sauces

As fleeting and as fiery as a bottle rocket, the pungency of horseradish blazes across the senses. Cooking destroys its explosively endearing qualities, so it is usually incorporated into uncooked sauces, relishes, and mayonnaises. Most often combined with whipped or sour cream for roast beef or smoked fish, horseradish is also endemic to tomato-based sauces for shellfish, creamy salad dressings, and, grated, with gefilte fish at Passover.

The difference between purchased and homemade herb products is no more pronounced than with horseradish. Ideally one goes out to the garden and digs up a root when needed, storing it for no more than a week in the refrigerator. Short of that, you can either dig up or purchase a large number of roots at once and freeze them or grate them and cover with vinegar.

To freeze, scrub, then lightly scrape away the outer skin, cut in half, and remove the center core. Wrap thoroughly and freeze, using within 6 months.

To preserve large quantities in vinegar, prepare as for freezing, but then mince in a food processor. Stand back when you remove the lid. Pack the grated horseradish tightly in 1-cup jars, then cover with vinegar. Cap the jars and refrigerate for up to 6 months.

To make a basic horseradish cream sauce, simply combine 1 cup sour cream or crème fraîche with 1/4 cup fresh or preserved grated horseradish and season with salt and pepper. Adding 2 tablespoons minced fresh chives, 1 tablespoon Dijon mustard, and 1/2 cup whipped cream elevates the sauce to a status befitting the best cuts of beef. A low-fat version would use nonfat or low-fat plain yogurt or yogurt cheese (see page 23).

For salad dressing, combine 2 tablespoons nonfat or low-fat plain yogurt, 2 tablespoons mayonnaise, and 2 tablespoons fresh or preserved grated horseradish.

Herbs are not shy growers, overleaf, as my mother's new garden attests only one year after planting.

APPLE-HORSERADISH SAUCE

Makes about 2 cups

This is great with smoked duck sausage, bratwurst, or other handmade sausages as well as slices of grilled pork or duck breast.

1 pound tart apples, such as Granny Smith, peeled, cored, and finely chopped

¼ cup dry white wine or fresh cider

2 tablespoons grated horseradish

2 tablespoons nonfat or low-fat plain yogurt

2 tablespoons fresh lemon juice or white wine vinegar

1 tablespoon honey

Combine all the ingredients in a bowl and let stand for 30 minutes before serving to allow flavors to blend.

HORSERADISH-TOMATO-ORANGE SALSA

Makes about 1 cup

Try this with grilled beef or fish, turkey scaloppine, or slices of poached chicken breast.

½ pound ripe tomatoes, peeled, and seeded (see page 31), then chopped (about 1 cup)

¼ cup thinly sliced scallions, both white and green parts

2 tablespoons grated horseradish

2 tablespoons champagne or white wine vinegar

¼ cup fresh orange juice

1 tablespoon grated orange zest

1 teaspoon sweet Hungarian paprika

¼ teaspoon hot red pepper sauce

Combine all the ingredients in a bowl and let stand for 30 minutes before serving to allow flavors to blend.

BOUQUET GARNI

French classical cooking formalized the practice of literally combining several herbs together in preparing a dish, giving it the name *bouquet garni*. The 1938 *Larousse Gastronomique* described this as "aromatic herbs or plants tied together into a little faggot." Bound by kitchen twine, button thread, or even unwaxed dental floss or trussed up in little bags, these bundles of herbs are removed prior to serving, leaving only their essence behind.

Bouquets garnis are particularly beneficent to stocks, sauces, stews, soups, dry beans, and steamed, poached, simmered, or baked vegetables or meats.

Parsley is almost always the central ingredient. Another two or three herbs are all that is necessary. Dried herbs and spices are fine to use too. Rather than being tied together, these are put into small muslin or paper tea bags (see Sources, page 150).

For fresh herbs, combine 2 or 3 fresh parsley sprigs and a sprig or leaf of each of the other herbs. For a dried bouquet garni, leave out the parsley and use 1/2 teaspoon of each of the herbs dried, plus a bay leaf, whole clove, allspice or juniper berry, peppercorns, or a bit of dried lemon or orange peel. Add fresh parsley near the end of cooking.

Possible bouquet garni combinations:
- Parsley, lovage, chives, and chervil
- Parsley, bay, and sage
- Parsley, mint, and garlic chives
- Parsley, lovage, marjoram, and bay
- Parsley, fennel, thyme, and bay
- Parsley, hyssop, and bay
- Parsley, tarragon, bay, and garlic chives
- Parsley, lemon thyme, bay, and savory
- Parsley, marjoram, thyme, and savory
- Parsley, rosemary, and sage
- Thyme, rosemary, oregano, and bay
- Fennel, dill, and bay

SALT-FREE HERB SEASONING

Makes about 3/4 cup

Another popular way to add a mixture of herbs and spices to foods is to use dried herb blends and herb-seasoned salts. Herb plants yield prodigious quantities, so there is often an abundance of dried herbs to utilize for these. What's nice about making your own is that you can control how the herbs were grown and what goes into the mixes. The downside is that you may end up with a lot of unused mixtures, which will lose flavor after 6 months. You're probably better off making small quantities of the bouquet garni described.

What I've found most useful for myself are salt-free herb seasonings that I sprinkle on foods when I'm just throwing a meal together, whether heating up a carryout, whipping up a vinaigrette, or seasoning some steamed vegetables before I stagger back to the computer.

¼ cup instant minced onion

¼ cup dried dill leaves

3 tablespoons toasted white sesame seeds (see page 70)

1 tablespoon dried thyme

2 teaspoons dried oregano

2 teaspoons celery seeds

2 teaspoons dried lemon peel

1 teaspoon sweet Hungarian paprika

½ teaspoon garlic powder

½ teaspoon freshly ground black pepper

Use a mortar and pestle, spice grinder, or coffee mill to grind all the ingredients together. Put into a shaker with large holes. Cap tightly.

HERB JELLIES AND JAMS

My first 6 years were spent in a rambling 100-year-old farmhouse that my parents had struggled to restore. That period ended one January when it burned to the ground. What I wanted to save that night were my books and my jelly. It's comforting to know that even at that tender age my priorities were already clear. Books and food are still key in my life, with jelly being a microcosm of my love for gardening and preserving its gifts in a form readily shared with family and friends.

Besides that, jellies and jams just plain taste good. From my dad I've learned the satisfaction of a piece of jelly bread for dessert. Mother has been making to-die-for pies and other goodies for him for over fifty years, but her jelly is still his favorite.

Melding my fascination with herbs with my pleasure in making and eating preserved fruit was a natural progression. Herbs heighten the quality of jellies and jams, lending intriguing, mysterious flavor. Whether you spread them on breakfast bread or tea scones, make a jelly cake roll, add them to sweet-and-sour sauces, or glaze vegetables and meats with them, jellies make foods taste better.

Herbs can be used singly or in combinations. Besides the suggestions given here, consider ones mentioned elsewhere in this book. The best way to find out how an herb and fruit might go together is simply to try them out, tasting a bit of fruit with a nibble of herb. Both fresh or dried herbs can be used. Many health food stores sell dried herbs in bulk for much less than grocery store cost. These stores also sell a mouth-watering assortment of organic juices. This means that both the herbs and the fruit juices are available year-round for jelly making.

There are several different ways to include herbs in jellies and jam. As with herbal vinegars, adding just a sprig to a jar for decoration is hardly worth the effort. To get maximum effect, use a lot of fresh herbs.

Because of time and energy limitations, a decision to eat less sugar, and the wide availability of no-sugar preserves, my favorite shortcut is to warm the contents of a jar of purchased sugarless preserves over low heat, adding 1/4 to 1/2 cup minced fresh herbs. As soon as the preserves can be stirred I remove it from the heat, let it cool slightly, pour it back into the jar, and refrigerate for several days before using.

A basic method for making herb jelly is to bring 6 cups water, fruit juice, or sweet wine to a boil over medium-high heat. Remove from the heat and stir in 1 to 2 cups loosely packed fresh herbs or 1/2 to 1 ounce dried herbs. Cover and let steep for at least 30 minutes. Use a strainer or paper coffee filter to strain out the herbs. Use this liquid to make jelly, following the directions on the packet of fruit pectin. New pectins are available that can jell either with no sugar or with artificial sweeteners, fruit juice concentrates, or reduced quantities of sugar. Brand names include Pomona's Universal Pectin, Slim Set, and Sure-Jell Light.

For herb jams, simply add 1 cup or more minced fresh herbs for every 3 cups fruit pulp in your favorite recipe.

Be bold in making homemade herb jellies and jams. Even when they "fail" and are runny, they become wonderfully flavored sauces to serve over ice cream, cake, pancakes, or poached fruit or to use as a glaze for meat. Food coloring can be added, but why not add edible flowers or fresh leaves instead?

There's really no reason why any herb can't be used to make jellies and jams, so brainstorm and explore.

Some combinations to try:

- Angelica with orange
- Angelica and sweet cicely with apple or strawberry
- Coriander leaves (cilantro) with peach or nectarine
- Lavender with cherry or orange
- Sweet woodruff with a late-harvest Riesling
- Sage with apple
- Rose petals with blush or rosé wine
- Ginger with cranberry
- Rose geranium with raspberry
- Basil with pineapple, peach, or tomato
- Marjoram with papaya
- Rosemary with apricot, citrus, or cranberry
- Savory or hyssop with pink grapefruit
- Thyme with grape
- Tarragon with blueberry
- Mint with strawberry or blackberry

HERB BUTTER

Makes about 1 ¼ cups

Once the darling of herb gardeners, herb butters have certainly lost their cachet in the concern over calories, dietary fat, cholesterol, factory farms, and pesticide contamination. This is not to diminish the unsurpassed flavor of fresh unsalted butter made from the milk of organically raised cows, especially Jerseys or Guernseys.

Ever mindful of the *m* word—moderation—we need not exclude such pleasures from our lives. Instead, I like to spread some herb butter occasionally on freshly baked bread or hot corn-on-the-cob, snuggle a bit into a mound of mashed potatoes, or whisk some into a *beurre blanc*. No doubt, you have your own preferred ways of indulging in butter.

Almost any herb or edible flower, either singly or in combination, can be used, as well as various liqueurs and citrus juices and zests. Minced onion or shallot and black olives are other possible inclusions. Formed into a log 1 1/2 inches thick, well wrapped, and frozen, herb butters preserve the essence of summer for fetes throughout the year.

1 cup (2 sticks) unsalted butter, at room temperature

*1 tablespoon fresh lemon juice, dry white wine,
dry vermouth, or liqueur*

¼ to ½ cup minced fresh herb leaves

1 teaspoon grated citrus zest (optional)

Cream the butter by hand or with a mixer, incorporating the lemon juice, herbs, and zest. Allow the flavors to blend for at least 2 hours before using. Refrigerate, using within 1 week, or freeze for up to 6 months.

HERB MUSTARD

Makes about 1 cup

In seventeenth-century England, mustard was eaten to enliven the spirit and improve memory as well as to accompany meat. No such claims are made today, but the thought of pretzels, vinaigrettes, or hot dogs, among other things, without mustard certainly makes me sad.

Fresh or dried herbs or spices can be added to prepared mustard, but starting from scratch with dry mustard achieves splendid results.

The best herbs for flavoring mustards include chives, coriander (cilantro), dill, garlic, green peppercorns, horseradish, mint, parsley, rosemary, sage, shallots, tarragon, and thyme, but try experimenting with others.

Shoyu is a Japanese soy sauce that is lower in salt; it is available at health food stores.

¼ cup yellow or brown mustard seeds

¼ cup dry mustard

½ cup hot water

½ cup white or red wine or other vinegar

¼ cup dry white wine, vermouth, or red wine, or beer

*1 to 2 tablespoons minced fresh herb leaves or
2 teaspoons freshly ground herb seeds*

1 teaspoon salt or shoyu

1 teaspoon honey

⅛ to ¼ teaspoon freshly ground black pepper

*⅛ to ¼ teaspoon ground spice, such as allspice, cinnamon,
or cloves*

½ teaspoon finely minced garlic or shallot

In a small bowl, combine the first 6 ingredients. Set aside for 3 hours. Pour the mixture into a food processor or blender and combine with the remaining ingredients, blending until a fine texture results.

Pour the mustard mixture into the top of a double boiler over simmering water on medium-high heat. Stirring, cook until thick but still thinner than prepared mustard, about 10 minutes. Cool, then pour into a jar, cap tightly, label, and refrigerate.

GRAPE-AND-CHERRY-LEAF DILL PICKLES

Makes 6 pints

In one form or another, I've been making these cucumber pickles with a grape leaf on top since I was a kid. Though it's often mentioned in older cookbooks, I've yet to read a good explanation for the grape leaf. Whatever the reason, these do have a unique flavor, which some people describe as grapelike, and the pickles are usually very crisp. The peppers, peppercorns, and cherry leaves are optional; the grape leaves, dill, and garlic are not. My own preference is to use dill heads rather than seeds because the result seems more summery.

Since the goal is to have lots of flowering heads of dill, the best variety for this use is 'Bouquet'. Gather and use the heads when the seeds have formed.

Even though these pickles are expeditiously prepared, try to give them at least a few months before sampling, because the flavors blend and improve with time.

6 fresh grape leaves

4 pounds thin, straight 4-inch-long pickling cucumbers

1 quart pure cider or other vinegar with 5-percent acidity

1 quart water

½ cup noniodized salt

12 black peppercorns

6 garlic cloves

12 fresh cherry leaves

6 small fresh or dried hot peppers or twelve ½-inch strips red bell pepper

6 heads fresh dill or 6 tablespoons dill seeds

Soak the grape leaves in cold water to cover overnight.

Prepare a boiling-water bath by filling a large deep canner or kettle with a canning rack and enough water to cover the jars by at least 1 inch. Turn the heat to high so that the water is boiling when the jars are ready for processing.

Wash the cucumbers, removing any stems or blossoms. If desired, cut into spears. Combine the vinegar, water, and salt in a medium-size saucepan over high heat, bringing to a boil and stirring until the salt is dissolved.

In each of 6 clean pint jars, place 2 peppercorns, 1 garlic clove, 2 cherry leaves, 1 hot pepper or 2 bell pepper strips, and 1 head fresh dill or 1 tablespoon dill seeds. Pack the jars with cucumbers. Fill the jars to within 1/2 inch of the top with the boiling pickling mixture. Put a drained grape leaf in each jar. Dry the jar rim with a towel and attach the canning lids securely.

Place the jars on the wire rack in the boiling-water bath. Cover. When the water returns to a rolling boil, time for 10 minutes, then remove the jars with a jar lifter. As the jars cool, the lids will "pop" and recess, signifying that they have sealed. If they don't pop, refrigerate and eat within 2 weeks.

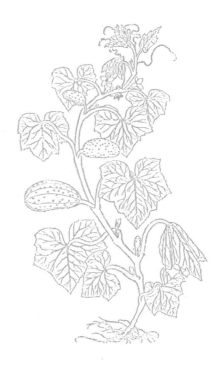

A cup of herb tea is a comforting tradition even though it consists of nothing more than fresh or dried leaves, flowers, seeds, or roots steeped in hot water. Almost as ancient is flavoring brandy or spirits with herbs. Many a medieval monastery or castle stillroom based its reputation on secret mixtures that might consist of more than a hundred herbs. Few of us are apt to take the time for anything so complicated, but using herbs in liqueurs as well as punches, shrubs, shakes, juleps, coolers, or mulled wine is just as satisfying today.

Especially pretty in any chilled drink are herb flowers in the ice cubes. Use any edible flower, such as borage, rose petals, mint, thyme, rose geranium, violets, or lavender. Put an individual flower or tiny sprig in each section of an ice cube tray. Half-fill with water. Freeze solidly, then fill completely with water. Ice rings for punch bowls can be made the same way.

Note: To substitute dried herbs for fresh, lessen quantities by one-half to two-thirds.

LEMONADE WITH MINT AND LEMON BALM

Makes 6 cups, about 8 servings

Part of the folklore of lemon balm is its traditional association with merriment and gaiety, and nothing can bring vitality to a languid body better than an iced glass of this old-fashioned lemony tonic. The hardest part of making it is choosing which mint to use. Try apple, blue balsalm, ginger, grapefruit, Japanese, lime, or orange mint as well as standard-issue spearmint or peppermint.

3 lemons, plus extra juice to taste if needed
1 orange
½ cup honey, or more to taste
½ cup minced fresh mint leaves
½ cup minced fresh lemon balm leaves
1 cup boiling water
1 quart cold water
Fresh mint and lemon balm sprigs

Peel the rind from the lemons and orange, being sure to avoid any of the bitter white pith. In a large heatproof pitcher or bowl, combine the lemon and orange peel, honey, mint, and lemon balm. Pour on the boiling water, and stir until the honey is blended in well. Allow to steep for 30 minutes. Strain and add the juice from the lemons and orange. Put into a pitcher and add the cold water. Add honey or lemon juice to taste. Chill for 1 hour. Serve over ice, garnished with the fresh herb sprigs.

RASPBERRY-LIME CRUSH WITH ANISE HYSSOP FLOWERS

Makes 6 cups, about 8 servings

The violet-blue flowers of the perennial anise hyssop make a magnificent display in the summer and fall garden. That they also bestow their sweet scent and flavor of anise and mint to foods is truly a gift. Easily grown 'Heritage' ever-bearing raspberries produce a significant crop of berries at the same time of year in the garden. Together they yield this lovely pink ambrosia.

¼ cup fresh anise hyssop flowers

¾ cup honey

3 cups boiling water

2 cups fresh lime juice (about 12 to 15 limes)

1 cup fresh raspberries

Fresh anise hyssop flower sprigs

Put the hyssop flowers and honey in a heatproof pitcher or bowl and pour the boiling water over them. Let cool for 30 minutes. Strain, then add the lime juice and raspberries. Cover and let steep for 2 hours in the refrigerator. Puree in 2 batches in a blender and serve over ice, garnished with additional hyssop flowers.

JUDY SCHAD'S FRUIT JUICE SHRUB

Makes 11 cups, or about 14 servings

No one is quite sure of the origin of the term *shrub*, although it may derive from the Arabic *sharāb*, which means drink. In colonial days a shrub combined fruit juices, sugar, and brandy or rum. Gradually the drink has evolved to where the alcohol has been replaced by vinegar, making it a second cousin to switchel, a traditional drink made with cider vinegar, molasses, and water. By whatever name, this old-fashioned concoction is sure to quench your thirst and beguile your palate.

Six 4-inch fresh sweet woodruff sprigs

4 or 5 fresh rose geranium leaves or 4 fresh mint sprigs

½ cup cider vinegar

½ cup honey or ¾ cup sugar

2 cups boiling water

1 quart cranberry juice

1 quart apple, grape, or pineapple juice

Combine the woodruff, geranium leaves, vinegar, and honey in a heatproof bowl. Add the boiling water, stir, and allow to steep for 30 minutes. Strain into a large pitcher. Stir in fruit juices. Chill before serving over ice. Make a fizzy drink by diluting with sparkling water when serving.

HERBED GINGERADE FIZZ

Makes 9 cups, about 12 servings

Peppery yet sweet, the flavor of ginger, along with its digestive qualities, has made it an herb synonymous with beverages through the millennia and around the world, whether in switchels, punches, ales, or beers. The base for this version can be kept in the refrigerator for about a week, then combined with the sparkling water when you're in need of a restorative.

½ pound fresh ginger, peeled and finely chopped

¼ cup minced fresh lemon balm and/or lemon verbena leaves

¼ cup minced fresh pineapple mint and/or grapefruit mint leaves

2 tablespoons grated lemon zest

½ cup honey

1 cup boiling water

3 cups fresh pineapple juice

1 cup fresh grapefruit juice

1 teaspoon pure vanilla extract

1 quart sparkling water

Combine the ginger, lemon balm, mint, and zest and tie in a cheesecloth bag. Place the bag in a heatproof pitcher or nonreactive bowl with the honey and pour in the boiling water. Stir and let steep for 30 minutes. Remove and discard the bag. Combine the ginger liquid with the pineapple and grapefruit juices and vanilla. To serve, fill a glass with ice, then half fill it with the gingerade, top off with sparkling water, and stir.

BERRY-MINT YOGURT SHAKE

Makes 2 servings

Considered an elixir of long life, yogurt is indeed a nourishing, readily assimilated food. Combined with berries and fruit juice, it becomes an energizing breakfast or rejuvenating nectar. Try different flavors of mint as well as other sweet herbs and flowers, such as angelica leaves, anise hyssop flowers, bergamot leaves and flowers, lavender flowers, rose petals, rose geranium leaves and flowers, sweet cicely leaves, and violet flowers.

1 cup ice-cold fruit juice or water

1 cup nonfat or low-fat plain yogurt

½ cup fresh or thawed frozen strawberries, raspberries, or blueberries

12 fresh mint leaves

Whole berries and fresh mint sprigs

Using a blender or food processor, combine the juice, yogurt, berries, and mint until smooth. Pour into glasses and garnish with fresh berries and mint sprigs.

The hand-hewn staves of these white-oak barrels imbue their contents with a special flavor.

FRUIT PUNCH
WITH HERBS

Make 10 cups, about 12 servings

Fresh herb leaves and flowers combined with fruit and plain or sparkling fruit juice, wine, or water yield glorious punches for all manner of occasions. Made with champagne and a vintage wine, then served in an antique cut-glass punch bowl ringed with flowers, this punch is fitting for the most elegant of parties. If you're feeling virtuous, try organic apple juice and sparkling water. For a Thanksgiving or Christmas feast, use sparkling cranberry juice. Sparkling raspberry juice would be perfect for a summertime gathering.

Experiment with various herbs, used singly or in combinations of no more than four or five herbs. Try rose geranium, sage, lemon balm, and rosemary with strawberries and wine or rosemary with strawberries, lemon and lime juices, and sparkling water. Sweet woodruff with strawberries, sweet white wine, and champagne makes May wine. Be sure to consider lemon balm, borage, lemons, and wine; rose geranium, apple juice, and limes; lemon verbena, mint, sage, rosemary, and rose geranium with strawberries and wine; or lemon balm, borage, mint, lemons, and oranges with pineapple juice and ginger ale.

½ cup fresh herb leaves and flowers
½ cup honey

3 cups boiling water; 1 fifth dry white, blush, or rosé wine; or 3 cups fruit juice

2 fifths chilled sparkling wine, or 32-ounce bottles of sparkling water or ginger ale

Fresh fruit such as strawberries, orange slices, or kiwifruit slices

Edible flowers such as fresh borage, scented geranium, anise hyssop, roses, rosemary, sweet woodruff, or violet

Put the herbs and honey in a heatproof bowl or pitcher. Pour the boiling water over them, stir and let steep for 30 minutes. If you're using wine or fruit juice instead, let steep for at least 6 hours or overnight in the refrigerator. Strain. Pour into a punch bowl or large pitcher and add sparkling water. Add fresh fruit and edible flowers.

MINT JULEP

Makes 1 serving

Made by the gallon on the first Saturday of May at Churchill Downs for the running of the Kentucky Derby, the mint julep has a heritage dating back at least to the the early nineteenth century. From the beginning there has been much discourse on the proper procedure and proportions. My favorite is that of Henry Watterson, a newspaper editor from Louisville, who, around 1910, wrote, "Pluck the mint gently from its bed, just as the dew of the evening is about to form upon it. Select the choicer sprigs only, but do not rinse them. Prepare the simple syrup and measure out a half-tumbler of whiskey. Pour the whiskey into a well-frosted silver cup, throw the other ingredients away and drink the whiskey."

The goal is to achieve a proper balance among the flavors of bourbon, mint, and sugar, with none dominating. Use only the best Kentucky bourbon, such as Maker's Mark, and, of course, 'Kentucky Colonel' mint.

John Egerton's book *Southern Food*, a definitive volume on the history of food in the South as well as how to cook it at home, provides the basis for this recipe.

1 teaspoon sugar

1 teaspoon water

5 or 6 large fresh mint leaves

Crushed ice

2 ounces Kentucky bourbon

Fresh mint sprig

Put the sugar, water, and mint leaves in the bottom of a glass. Mash with a spoon until the sugar is dissolved and the essense of the mint is extracted. Fill the glass with ice. When frost forms on the outside, slowly pour in the bourbon, letting it trickle through the ice, then stir. Garnish with a sprig of mint and serve immediately.

RED WINE-HERB COOLER

Makes 12 cups, about 16 servings

In John Gerard's 1597 herbal, borage was extolled for comforting the heart, driving away sorrow, and increasing the joy of the mind. Surely a glass of this cheerful red wine cooler, replete with the blithe blue flowers of borage, would cause one to leave care behind.

4 fresh borage leaves

Twelve 4-inch fresh salad burnet sprigs

6 fresh lemon verbena or lemon balm leaves

1 cup fresh orange juice

½ cup fresh lemon juice

½ cup brandy or orange liqueur

½ cup honey

2 fifths dry red wine

One 32-ounce bottle sparkling water

Fresh borage flowers

In a large bowl or pitcher, combine the borage, burnet, lemon verbena, orange and lemon juices, brandy, and honey. Stir and chill for 6 hours or overnight. Strain and combine with the wine and sparkling water. Serve over ice with fresh borage flowers for garnish.

MULLED WINE WITH SPICES AND ROSEMARY

Makes 9 cups, about 12 servings

Most likely the practice of heating wine with herbs, spices, and fruits began as a means of disguising a poor-quality vintage, but now it has a much more romantic connotation. Mulled wine evokes images of blazing fires, winter holiday outings, and silently falling snow. It can make any gathering a party and is the perfect accompaniment to an afternoon spent baking cookies.

2 bottles dry red wine

2 cups brewed Earl Grey tea

2 cups cranberry juice

1 cup fresh orange juice

½ cup orange liqueur

½ cup honey

2 oranges, seeded and thinly sliced

Two 3-inch cinnamon sticks, broken into pieces

8 whole cloves

Seeds from 4 whole cardamom pods

Four 3-inch fresh rosemary sprigs

Additional 3-inch cinnamon sticks for stirrers

In a large heavy nonreactive pot, combine the wine, tea, cranberry and orange juices, liqueur, honey, and orange slices. Tie the broken cinnamon sticks, cloves, cardamom seeds, and rosemary together in a cheesecloth bag and add to the wine mixture. Over medium heat, bring the mixture just to a boil, then reduce the heat to low, cover, and simmer for 30 minutes. Ladle into mugs or punch cups, adding cinnamon sticks as stirrers.

Mulled wine can be set aside and reheated several hours later or refrigerated and reheated the next day. Replace the orange slices with fresh ones.

HERB LIQUEURS

Makes about 1 quart

For many centuries herbs were looked upon more for their health benefits than for their culinary efficacy. One of the common ways of deriving the healthful property of an herb was to steep it in a strong spirit, such as brandy, vodka, or eau-de-vie. Everything from melancholia to bubonic plague was thought to be remedied by such herbal infusions. One wonders how much the populace longed to be ill just for the cure.

Herbs to use in liqueurs include angelica, anise, bay, caraway, coriander, cumin, fennel, hyssop, lavender, lemon balm, lemon verbena, mint, rose, rosemary, saffron, sage, sweet cicely, sweet woodruff, tarragon, thyme, and violet.

1 fifth vodka, brandy, rum, whiskey, or pure grain alcohol

2 to 3 cups fresh herb leaves and/or flowers or
½ cup lightly crushed angelica, anise, caraway, cumin, coriander, or fennel seeds

One or more of the following:
one 3-inch cinnamon stick, 3 allspice berries, 3 black peppercorns, 3 whole cloves, 1 star anise, 1 cardamom pod

Zest of 1 lemon, lime, tangerine, grapefruit, or orange (optional)
one cup honey, or 1½ cups sugar
½ cup water

Combine the chosen alcohol, herbs, seeds, spices, and citrus peel in a large glass jar with a tight-fitting lid or cork. Let steep in a dark, warm place for 4 to 6 weeks.

In a saucepan, combine the honey and water and cook over medium heat, stirring, until the honey is completely blended in and the mixture is warm. Cool to lukewarm. Strain the steeped alcohol mixture and combine with the sugar syrup. Rebottle and let mature for several more weeks. Decant into your prettiest decanters or bottles, giving some away as gifts if you can bear to part with any.

Selected Sources of Herb Seeds, Plants, Products, and Supplies

Abundant Life Seed Foundation
P. O. Box 772
Port Townsend, WA 98368
Catalogue $1.00; open-pollinated, fungicide-free seeds of heirloom herbs and other plants; books; public garden

Ahren's Nursery Herbal Country
Route 1
Huntingburg, IN 47542
Herb plants, strawberries, fruits and perennial vegetables

Alyce's Herb & Gourmet Herb Vinegars
1901 West Beltline Highway,
Box 9563
Madison, WI 53715
Catalogue $1.00; organic herbal vinegars and oils; public garden

Antique Rose Emporium
Route 5, Box 143
Brenham, TX 77833
Catalogue $5.00; antique and heirloom roses, perennials and perennial herb plants; books; public garden

Blue Springs
236 Eleanor Avenue
Los Altos, CA 94022
Catalogue $2.00; herb plants and seeds; dried herbs, spices, blends and vinegars

W. Atlee Burpee & Company
300 Park Avenue
Warminster, PA 18974
General supplier of vegetable, flower, herb and fruit seeds and plants; garden supplies

Cactus Patch Herbs
Route 2, Box 33
Seymour, IN 47274
Catalogue for SASE; organically grown herbs and flowers

Camelot Herb Gardens
245 Red Schoolhouse Road
Coventry, RI 02816
Catalogue $2.00; herb plants; dried herbs, spices and herbal products

Caprilands Herb Farm
534 Silver Sreet
Coventry, CT 06238
Herbal products; public garden

Capriole
10329 Newcut Road
Greenville, IN 47124
Fresh and aged goat cheeses

Carroll Gardens
P. O. Box 310
Westminster, MD 21157
Catalogue $3.00; perennials, herbs, roses, shrubs and trees

Chili Pepper Emporium
328 San Felipe N.W.
Albuquerque, NM 87104
Pepper seeds; dried herbs, chilis, chili wreaths, ristras and pepper products

Circle Herb Farm
Route 1, Box 247
East Jordan, MI 49727
Large variety of herb plants; fresh cut herbs; edible flowers

Clark's Greenhouse & Herbal Country
Route 1, Box 15B
San Jose, IL 62682
Catalogue $1.00; wide variety of herb plants and flowers; dried herbs; herb crafts; public garden; classes

Clement Herb Farm
Route 6, Box 390
Rogers, AR 72756
Catalogue $1.00; herb products; public garden

Companion Plants
7247 North Coolville Ridge Road
Athens, OH 45701
Catalogue $2.00; large list of herb and flower plants and seeds; public garden

The Cook's Garden
Box 535
Londonderry, VT 05148
Catalogue $1.00; herb, edible flower, vegetable and salad green seeds; gardening supplies; books

Country Heritage Nurseries
P. O. Box 536
Hartford, MI 49057
Fruit and perennial vegetable plants, shallots, garlic, horseradish and lemon grass

The Country Merchants
Route 2, Box 199
Cheney, KS 67025-9659
Catalogue $3.00; dried herbs, spices, products and supplies

The Country Shepherd
Route 1, Box 107
Comer, GA 30629
Catalogue $1.00; fresh and dried herbs and flowers; public garden

Dabney Herbs
Box 22061
Louisville, KY 40252-0061
Over 200 herb plant varieties, also some roses and herb seeds

DeGiorgi Seed Company
6011 N Street
Omaha, NE 68117
Catalogue $2.00; Herb, vegetable and flower seeds; garden art; books; supplies

Filaree Farm
Route 1, Box 162
Okanogan, WA 98840
Over 50 different garlic strains

The Flowery Branch
P. O. Box 1330
Flowery Branch, CA 30542
*Catalogue $2.00; large list of herb,
pepper, everlasting and flower seeds*

Forestfarm
990 Tetherow Road
Williams, OR 97544-9599
*Catalogue $3.00; very large selection
of herbs, perennials, everlastings, roses,
trees and shrubs*

Fox Hill Farm
P. O. Box 9
Parma, MI 49269-0009
Catalogue $1.00; large selection of herbs

Fox Hollow Herb & Heirloom
Seed Company
P. O. Box 148
McGrann, PA 16236
*Catalogue $1.00; herb, flower and
vegetable seeds in small and large
packets; books*

Fragrant Fields
128 Front Street
Dongola, IL 62926
*Herb, everlasting and flower plants;
dried herbs and flowers; herb products;
books; public garden*

The Gathered Herb
12114 North State Road
Otisville, MI 48463
*Catalogue $2.00; herb, perennial and
everlasting plants; herb products*

Glade Valley Nursery
9226 Links Road
Walkersville, MD 21793
*Catalogue $2.00; herb, perennial and
everlasting plants*

Good Seed Company
Star Route Box 73A
Oroville, WA 98844
*Catalogue $1.00; unusual selection of
herb, vegetable and everlasting seeds
and garlic*

Goodwin Creek Gardens
P. O. Box 83
Williams, OR 97544
*Catalogue $1.00; organically grown
herb, everlasting and fragrant plants;
herb seeds*

The Gourmet Gardener
4000 West 126th Street
Leawood, KS 66209
*Herb and vegetable seeds; books;
herb supplies*

Great Lakes Herb Company
Box 6713
Minneapolis, MN 55406
*Catalogue $1.00; organic dried herbs;
large list of herb products; herb seeds*

Greenmantle Nursery
3010 Ettersburg Road
Garberville, CA 95440
*Catalogue $3.00; organically grown
old-fashioned roses and old and unusual
fruit varieties*

Hartman's Herb Farm
Old Dana Road
Barre, MA 01005
*Catalogue $2.00; large selection of
herb and perennial plants; dried herbs,
spices and blends; herb products and
supplies; public garden*

Hastings, Seedsman to the South
1036 White Street, S.W.
Atlanta, GA 30310-8535
*Organically grown herb plants, seeds,
vegetables and flowers; books;
gardening supplies*

Havasu Hills Herbs
20150 Rough & Ready Trail
Sonora, CA 95370
Catalogue $1.00; herb plants and seeds

Hedgehog Hill Farm
Route 2, Box 2010
Buckfield, ME 04220-9549
*Catalogue $1.00; organically grown
dried herbs and herb products;
public garden*

Heirloom Garden Seeds
P. O. Box 138
Guerneville, CA 95446
Catalogue $2.50; herb seeds

The Herb Bar
200 West Mary
Austin, TX 78704
*Dried herbs; herb jars and drying racks;
herb products and supplies*

The Herb Garden
P. O. Box 773
Pilot Mountain, NC 27041-0773
*Catalogue $3.00; offers several hundred
herb plants; oils; dried herbs*

Herbal Effect
616 Lighthouse
Monterey, CA 93940
*Catalogue $2.00; herb products
and supplies*

The Herbary & Stuff
Route 3, Box 83
Jacksonville, TX 75766
Catalogue $2.00; herb, flower and pepper plants

The Herbfarm
32804 Issaquah-Fall City Road
Fall City, WA 98024
Catalogue $3.50; more than 600 herbs and related plants; herb products and supplies; public garden

Herbs-Liscious
1702 South Sixth Street
Marshalltown, IA 50158
Catalogue $2.00; herb plants; dried herbs; herb products; custom-growing service

Hidden Springs Herbs
Route 14, Box 159
Cookeville, TN 38501
Price list for SASE; good selection of herb plants

High Altitude Gardens
P. O. Box 4619
Ketchum, ID 83340
Catalogue $2.00; herb, vegetable and native plant seeds; books; gardening supplies

Hilltop Herb Farm
P. O. Box 325
Romayor, TX 77368
Herb plants and seeds; gourmet herbal foods

The Hollow, Orchids & Herbs
71 German Crossroad
Ithaca, NY 14850
Herb list for SASE; good selection of herb plants

Hortico, Inc.
723 Robson Road
Waterdown, Ontario
Canada L0R 2H1
Catalogue $2.00; hundreds of roses, herbs, perennials and other plants

Horticultural Enterprises
P. O. Box 810082
Dallas, TX 75381-0082
Large selection of pepper seed, plus some Mexican herbs and vegetables

J. L. Hudson, Seedsman
P. O. Box 1058
Redwood City, CA 94064
Catalogue $1.00; rare and unusual open-pollinated seeds of herbs and many other plants

Hundley Ridge Farm
Box 253, Squiresville Road
Perry Park, KY 40363
Herb, everlasting and perennial plants; baskets and herb markers

In Harmony with Nature
Route 1, Box 109
Rockton, PA 15856-0040
Catalogue $3.00; hundreds of herb and perennial plants; herb and natural food products; books; organic supplies

It's About Thyme
P. O. Box 878
Manchaca, TX 78652
Catalogue $1.00; large selection of herb and everlasting plants

Johnny's Selected Seeds
Foss Hill Raod
Albion, ME 04910
General supplier of herb, vegetable and flower seeds; garden supplies

Kingfisher, Inc.
P. O. Box 75
Wexford, PA 15090-0075
Catalogue $2.00; herb seeds and seed collections

Kinsman Company
River Road
Point Pleasant, PA 18950
Double-walled cold frame and gardening tools

A Kiss of the Sun Nursery
5273 South Coast Highway
South Beach, OR 97366
Catalogue $1.00; large selection of herb plants; books

Krystal Wharf Farms
Route 2, Box 2112
Mansfield, PA 16933
Organically grown vegetables, dried herbs and garden seeds

Lavender Lane
6715 Donerail Drive
Sacramento, CA 95842
Catalogue $2.00; wide range of containers for vinegars and other herbal products; empty tea and muslin bags

Legacy Herbs
HC 70, Box 442
Mountain View, AR 72560
Catalogue $.50; herb, everlasting and miniature rose plants; herb jellies, vinegars and other products

Le Jardin du Gourmet
P. O. Box 275
St. Johnsbury Center, VT 05863
Catalogue $.50; herb plants; shallot, garlic and onion sets; herb, vegetable and everlasting seeds; gourmet foods; books

Lewis Mountain Herbs &
Everlastings
2345 Street, Route 247
Manchester, OH 45144
*Herbs and everlasting plants; books;
public garden*

Lily of the Valley Herb Farm
3969 Fox Avenue
Minerva, OH 44657
*Catalogue $2.00; almost 600 herbs,
everlastings, perennials and other
plants; herbal products; books*

Logee's Greenhouses
141 North Street
Danielson, CT 06239
*Catalogue $3.00; tender plants, herbs
and scented geraniums; greenhouses
open to visitors*

Lowelands Farm
Route 1, Box 98
Middleburg, VA 22117
*Price list for SASE; organically grown
herbs used to make herbal vinegars,
cooking sherry, honeys and other items*

Mari-Mann Herb Company
Route 4, Box 7
Decatur, IL 62521-9404
*Catalogue $1.00; herb products and
supplies; public garden*

McClure & Zimmerman
P. O. Box 368
Friesland, WI 53935-0368
*Saffron crocus, garlics, chives
and shallots*

Mendocino Arts & Gifts
P. O. Box 1063
Mendocino, CA 95460-1063
*Catalogue $2.00; herb blends, oils,
vinegars, jellies and mustards and
garlic braids*

Merlin of the Rogue Valley
P. O. Box 1340
Merlin, OR 97532
*Herb vinegars, mustards, jellies
and blends*

Merry Gardens
P. O. Box 595
Camden, ME 04843-0595
*Catalogue $1.00; large selection of
herb plants*

Native Seeds/SEARCH
2509 North Campbell #325
Tucson, AZ 85719
*Catalogue $1.00; herb seeds related to
the Southwest*

The Natural Gardening Company
217 San Anselmo Avenue
San Anselmo, CA 94960
*Organically grown herb, vegetable and
flower plants; environmentally sound
gardening supplies*

New England Cheesemaking
Supply Company, Inc.
85 Main Street
Ashfield, MA 01330
*Catalogue $1.00; supplies for making
homemade cheese and yogurt*

Nichols Garden Nursery
1190 North Pacific Highway
Albany, OR 97321-4598
*Large selection of herb seeds and
plants, vegetable and flower seeds; herb
products; garden and kitchen supplies*

No Common Scents
Kings Yard
Yellow Springs, OH 45387
Dried herbs, spices and products

Old Southwest Trading Company
P. O. Box 7545
Albuquerque, NM 87194
*Large selection of dried chilis, ristras,
Southwestern foods, herbs and spices*

Geo. W. Park Seed Company
Cokesbury Road
Greenwood, SC 29647-0001
*General supplier of flower, herb,
vegetable and fruit seeds and plants;
gardening supplies*

Peace Seeds
2835 S.E. Thompson Street
Corvallis, OR 97333
*Catalogue $3.50; organically grown
heirloom and rare seeds of herbs,
flowers, vegetables and trees*

Pecos Valley Spice Co.
500 East 77th Street
New York, NY 10162
*Mexican herbs, spices and foods;
ground and crushed chilis*

Pendery's
304 East Belknap Street
Ft. Worth, TX 76102
*Catalogue $2.00; large selection of
culinary herbs, spices and blends,
including various hot peppers*

Penny's Garden
P. O. Box 305
Mountain City, GA 30562-0305
*Gourmet herbal foods, including jellies,
vinegars and mustards; public garden*

The Pepper Gal
P. O. Box 12534
Lake Park, FL 33403-0534
Price list for SASE; pepper seeds

Perseus Gourmet Products
1425 East Third
Kennewick, WA 99336
Brochure for SASE; organically grown herbs used in vinegars and oils; dried and fresh herbs

Pinetree Garden Seeds
Route 100
New Gloucester, ME 04260
Large selection of vegetables, herbs and flowers offered in small packets; garlic; garden and kitchen supplies; large selection of books

Plants of the Southwest
Agua Fria, Route 6, Box 11
Santa Fe, NM 87501
Catalogue $1.50; seeds and plants of heirloom and modern herbs, vegetables, flowers, trees, shrubs and other plants suited for arid as well as other climates

Rasland Farm
NC 82 at US 13
Godwin, NC 28344-9712
Catalogue $2.50; very large selection of herb plants; extensive assortment of herb products and supplies; dried herbs and blends; bouquet garni

Redwood City Seed Company
P. O. Box 361
Redwood City, CA 94064
Catalogue $1.00; extensive list of unusual seed of plants from around the world, pepper seed and garlic and shallot sets

Rabbit Shadow Farm
2880 East Highway 402
Loveland, CO 80537
Catalogue $1.00; herb topiaries, herbs and antique roses

Rafal Spice Company
2521 Russell Street
Detroit, MI 48207
Large list of herbs, spices, oils, extracts, containers, labels, reusable tea bags and other related products and supplies

G. B. Ratto & Co. International Grocers
821 Washington Street
Oakland, CA 94607
Specialty foods, including herbs, spices, oils, vinegars, crystallized flowers, products and supplies

Richters
Box 26
Goodwood, Ontario
Canada L0C 1A0
Catalogue $2.50; very large selection of herb seeds and plants; dried herbs and herb products; books; garden supplies

Rose Hill Herbs and Perennials
Route 4, Box 377
Amherst, VA 24521
Catalogue $2.00; extensive selection of herb plants

The Rosemary House
120 South Market Street
Mechanicsburg, PA 17055
Catalogue $2.00; large selection of herb plants and seeds; herb products and supplies; books; public garden

St. John's Herb Garden, Inc.
7711 Hillmeade Road
Bowie, MD 20720
Catalogue $5.00; herb, vegetable and flower seeds; large selection of dried herbs, spices and herbal products; books; public garden

Sandy Mush Herb Nursery
Route 2, Surrett Cove Road
Leicester, NC 28748
Catalogue $4.00; large selection of herb seeds and plants, also vegetable and everlasting seeds; books

Seeds Blum
Idaho City Stage
Boise, ID 83706
Catalogue $3.00; heirloom flower, vegetable and herb seeds; books

Select Origins, Inc.
Box N
Southampton, NY 11968
Dried herbs, spices, blends, garlic, vinegar and other specialty foods

Shady Hill Gardens
821 Walnut Street
Batavia, IL 60510
Catalogue $2.00; scented geraniums

Shepherd's Garden Seeds
6116 Highway 9
Felton, CA 95018
Catalogue $1.00; gourmet vegetable and herb seeds, also edible, everlasting and cutting flower seeds

Southern Exposure Seed Exchange
P. O. Box 158
North Garden, VA 22959
Price list for SASE, catalogue $3.00; heirloom varieties of vegetable, herb and flower seeds, including many peppers; unusual onions and shallots

Spice It Up
135 Amory Street
Cambridge, MA 02139
Custom-milled herbs, spices and blends

Spices 'N Things
6485 West 1000 South
South Whitley, IN 46787-9747
*Catalogue $1.00; dried herbs and
spices; herb products and supplies*

Stokes Seeds, Inc.
P. O. Box 548
Buffalo, NY 14240
*General supplier of vegetable, herb and
flower seeds; garden supplies*

Story House Herb Farm
Route 7, Box 246
Murray, KY 42071
*Catalogue $2.00; organically grown
herb plants*

Sugar 'n Spice
2819 Willow Street Pike
Willow Street, PA 17584
*Catalogue $1.75; dried herbs and
spices; herb products*

Sunnybrook Farms Nursery
9448 Mayfield Road
Chesterland, OH 44026
*Catalogue $1.00; herb and perennial
plants; dried herbs; books*

Sunrise Enterprises
P. O. Box 330058
West Hartford, CT 06133-0058
*Catalogue $2.00; Asian vegetables
and herbs*

Taylor's Herb Gardens, Inc.
1535 Lone Oak Road
Vista, CA 92084
*Catalogue $3.00; large selection of
herb seeds and plants; garlic*

Territorial Seed Company
P. O. Box 157
Cottage Grove, OR 97451
*Herb, vegetable and flower seeds;
garden supplies*

Tinmouth Channel Farm
Box 428B, Town Highway 19
Tinmouth, VT 05773
*Catalogue $2.00; organically grown
herb seeds and plants*

Triple Oaks Nursery
Route 47
Franklinville, NJ 08322
*Catalogue for SASE; wide selection of
herb plants and dried herbs*

The Ultimate Herb & Spice
Shoppe
111 Azalea, Box 395
Duenweg, MO 64841-0395
*Catalogue $2.00; dried herbs, spices
and blends; kitchen and herb products
and supplies; organic grains*

United Society of Shakers—
Herb Department
Route 1, Box 640
Poland Spring, ME 04274
*Price list for SASE; rose water,
vinegars and other herb products*

Vermont Bean Seed Company
Garden Lane
Fair Haven, VT 05743
*Excellent selection of vegetable and
herb seeds*

Vileniki—An Herb Farm
Route 1, Box 345
Olyphant, PA 18447
*Catalogue $1.50; large selection of
herb plants*

Washington National Cathedral
Wisconsin and Massachusetts
Avenues
Washington, DC 20016-5098
*Brochure $1.00; herb plants;
public garden*

Wayside Gardens
1 Garden Lane
Hodges, SC 19695-0001
*Large selection of flowers, shrubs, trees,
roses and herbs*

Weisenberger Mills
P. O. Box 215
Midway, KY 40357
Flours and mixes

Paprikas Weiss Importer
1546 Second Avenue
New York, NY 10028
*Catalogue $3.00; herbs, spices, vinegars,
oils, unusual foods and kitchenware*

Well-Sweep Herb Farm
317 Mt. Bethel Road
Port Murray, NJ 07865
*Catalogue $2.00; large selection of
herb plants and seeds; herb products
and supplies; books; public garden*

Westwind Seeds
2509 North Campbell, #139
Tucson, AZ 85719
*Excellent selection of open-pollinated,
chemically untreated vegetable, herb
and flower seeds*

Windy River Farm/Cottage
Garden Herbs
P. O. Box 312
Merlin, OR 97532
*Catalogue $1.00; certified organic farm
with dried herbs, blends, vinegars,
honeys and unsulfured, dried fruits
and vegetables*

Wrenwood of Berkeley Springs
Route 4, Box 361
Berkeley Springs, WV 25411-9413
*Catalogue $2.00; large selection of
herb plants, perennials and everlastings;
public garden*

Selected Reading

Barton, Barbara J. GARDENING BY MAIL: A SOURCE BOOK. Boston: Houghton Mifflin, 1990.

Bonar, Ann. THE MACMILLAN TREASURY OF HERBS. New York: Macmillan, 1985.

Bremness, Lesley. THE COMPLETE BOOK OF HERBS. New York: Viking Penguin, 1988.

Brody, Jane. JANE BRODY'S GOOD FOOD GOURMET. New York: W. W. Norton, 1990.

Burros, Marian. KEEP IT SIMPLE: 30-MINUTE MEALS FROM SCRATCH. New York: William Morrow, 1981.

Choate, Judith. GOURMET PRESERVES. New York: Grove Weidenfeld, 1987.

Creasy, Rosalind. COOKING FROM THE GARDEN. San Francisco: Sierra Club Books, 1988.

Cunningham, Marion. THE FANNIE FARMER COOKBOOK. New York: Alfred A. Knopf, 1991.

The East West Journal, eds. SHOPPER'S GUIDE TO NATURAL FOODS. Garden City Park, NY: Avery Publishing Group, 1987.

Egerton, John. SOUTHERN FOOD. New York: Alfred A. Knopf, 1987.

Ferrary, Jeannette and Louise Fiszer. SEASON TO TASTE. New York: Simon and Schuster, 1988.

Foster, Gertrude B. and Rosemary F. Louden. PARK'S SUCCESS WITH HERBS. Greenwood, SC: Geo. W. Park Seed Co., 1980.

Garden Way Publishing, eds. HERBS: 1001 GARDENING QUESTIONS ANSWERED. Pownal, VT: Storey Communications, 1990.

Greene, Bert. THE GRAINS COOKBOOK. New York: Workman Publishing, 1988.

— — —. GREENE ON GREENS. New York: Workman Publishing, 1984.

Herbst, Sharon Tyler. FOOD LOVER'S COMPANION. New York: Barron's, 1990.

Horn, Jane, ed. COOKING A TO Z. San Ramon, CA: Chevron Chemical Company, 1988.

Hutson, Lucinda. THE HERB GARDEN COOKBOOK. Austin, TX: Texas Monthly Press, 1987.

Jordan, Julie. WINGS OF LIFE VEGETARIAN COOKERY. Trumansburg, NY: The Crossing Press, 1976.

Kilham, Christopher S. THE BREAD & CIRCUS WHOLE FOOD BIBLE. Reading, MA: Addison-Wesley, 1991.

Kowalchik, Claire & William H. Hylton, Editors. RODALE'S ILLUSTRATED ENCYCLOPEDIA OF HERBS. Emmaus, PA: Rodale Press, 1987.

Lathrop, Norma Jean. HERBS: HOW TO SELECT, GROW AND ENJOY. Tucson: HPBooks, 1981.

Lemlin, Jeanne. VEGETARIAN PLEASURES. New York: Alfred A. Knopf, 1986.

Lima, Patrick. THE HARROWSMITH ILLUSTRATED BOOK OF HERBS. Camden East, Ontario: Camden House, 1986.

— — —. THE NATURAL FOOD GARDEN. Rockling, CA: Prima Publishing, 1992.

Luard, Elisabeth. THE OLD WORLD KITCHEN. New York: Bantam Books, 1987.

Madison, Deborah with Edward Espe Brown. THE GREENS COOK BOOK. New York: Bantam Books, 1987.

Madison, Deborah. THE SAVORY WAY. New York: Bantam Books, 1990.

Martin, Tovah. THE ESSENCE OF PARADISE. Boston: Little, Brown, 1991.

McGee, Harold. ON FOOD AND COOKING. New York: Macmillan, 1984.

McRae, Bobbi A. THE HERB COMPANION WISHBOOK AND RESOURCE GUIDE. Loveland, CO: Interweave Press, 1992.

Miller, Amy Bess and Persis Fuller. THE BEST OF SHAKER COOKING. New York: Collier Books, 1970.

Minnich, Jerry. GARDENING FOR MAXIMUM NUTRITION. Emmaus, PA: Rodale Press, 1983.

The National Gardening Association, eds. GARDENING: THE COMPLETE GUIDE TO GROWING AMERICA'S FAVORITE FRUITS & VEGETABLES. Reading, MA: Addison-Wesley, 1986.

Newcomb, Duane and Karen Newcomb. THE COMPLETE VEGETABLE GARDENER'S SOURCEBOOK. New York: Prentice Hall, 1989.

Newdick, Jane. BETTY CROCKER'S BOOK OF FLOWERS. New York: Prentice Hall, 1989.

Ogden, Shepherd and Ellen Ogden. THE COOK'S GARDEN. Emmaus, PA: Rodale Press, 1989.

Owen, Millie. A COOK'S GUIDE TO GROWING HERBS, GREENS & AROMATICS. New York: Alfred A. Knopf, 1981.

Painter, Gilian. A HERB COOKBOOK. Auckland: Hodder and Stoughton, 1983.

Pellegrini, Angelo M. THE FOOD-LOVER'S GARDEN. Seattle: Madrona Publishers, 1970.

Piercy, Caroline. THE SHAKER COOKBOOK. New York: Weathervane Books, 1986.

Plagemann, Catherine. FINE PRESERVING. Annotated by M. F. K. Fisher. Berkeley: Aris Books, 1986.

Roehl, Evelyn. WHOLE FOOD FACTS. Rochester, VT: Healing Arts Press, 1988.

Rogers, Jean. COOKING WITH THE HEALTHFUL HERBS. Emmaus, PA: Rodale Press, 1983.

Rohe, Fred. THE COMPLETE BOOK OF NATURAL FOODS. Boulder, CO: Shambhala Press, 1983.

Shepherd, Renee. RECIPES FROM A KITCHEN GARDEN. Felton, CA: Shepherd's Garden Publishing, 1987.

——— and Fran Raboff. RECIPES FROM A KITCHEN GARDEN. VOL. 2. Felton, CA: Shepherd's Garden Publishing, 1991.

Sinnes, A. Cort. THE GRILLING BOOK. Berkeley, CA: Aris Books, 1985.

Stobart, Tom. HERBS, SPICES AND FLAVOURINGS. New York: Viking Penguin, 1987.

Tannahill, Reay. FOOD IN HISTORY. New York: Stein and Day. 1973.

Thorne, John. AGLIO, OGLIO, BASILICO. Boston: The Jackdaw Press, 1981.

Trewby, Mary. A GOURMET'S GUIDE TO HERBS & SPICES. Los Angeles, CA: HPBooks, 1989.

Vickers, Lois. THE SCENTED LAVENDER BOOK. Boston: Little, Brown, 1991.

Vongerichten, Jean-Georges. SIMPLE CUISINE. New York: Prentice Hall, 1990.

Walter, Eugene. HINTS & PINCHES. Atlanta: Longstreet Press, 1991.

Weitzel, Patricia, ed. HERBS: A COOKBOOK AND MORE. Cleveland: The Western Reserve Herb Society, 1979.

White, Susan, ed. WEISENBERGER COOKBOOK II. Midway, KY: Weisenberger Mills, 1988.

Wood, Rebecca. THE WHOLE FOODS ENCYCLOPEDIA: A SHOPPER'S GUIDE. New York: Prentice Hall, 1988.

Index